Supporting
New Teachers

For Mr. Calvin Wallace,
extraordinary visionary, leader, mentor, and friend.
I listened.

Supporting New Teachers

A How-To Guide for Leaders

Lynn F. Howard

Foreword by Lisa Parker

CORWIN
A SAGE Company

FOR INFORMATION:

Corwin
A SAGE Company
2455 Teller Road
Thousand Oaks, California 91320
(800) 233-9936
www.corwin.com

SAGE Publications Ltd.
1 Oliver's Yard
55 City Road
London EC1Y 1SP
United Kingdom

SAGE Publications India Pvt. Ltd.
B 1/I 1 Mohan Cooperative Industrial Area
Mathura Road, New Delhi 110 044
India

SAGE Publications Asia-Pacific Pte. Ltd.
3 Church Street
#10-04 Samsung Hub
Singapore 049483

Executive Editor: Arnis Burvikovs
Senior Associate Editor: Desirée A. Bartlett
Editorial Assistant: Andrew Olson
Production Editor: Melanie Birdsall
Copy Editor: Cate Huisman
Typesetter: C&M Digitals (P) Ltd.
Proofreader: Catherine Forrest
Indexer: Jean Casalegno
Cover Designer: Anupama Krishnan
Marketing Manager: Amy Vader

Printed in the United States of America

Library of Congress Cataloging-in-Publication Data

Howard, Lynn F.
Supporting new teachers : a how-to guide for leaders / Lynn F. Howard; foreword by Lisa Parker.

pages cm
Includes bibliographical references and index.

ISBN 978-1-4833-7500-7 (pbk. : alk. paper)

1. First year teachers—United States. 2. Teachers—In-service training—United States. 3. Teacher turnover—United States—Prevention. 4. Mentoring in education—United States. 5. Educational leadership—United States. I. Title.

LB2844.1.N4H693 2016

370.71'1—dc23   2015015422

This book is printed on acid-free paper.

15 16 17 18 19 10 9 8 7 6 5 4 3 2 1

Contents

Foreword

I would often play pretend school with my family and friends during my childhood. My teachers, at the end of the school year, would allow me to assist with the physical close out of the year. In return for my services, they would provide me with a copy of an attendance/gradebook, worksheets, writing instruments, books, and chalk. I was voted by my sister and cousins to be the family teacher, because they trusted me to demonstrate great teaching and to make it fun. This was the beginning of my teaching experiences and formative years of developing mentor relationships. My teachers would say to me, "One day you will become an outstanding educator," I became a middle and high school mathematics teacher in Virginia Beach Public Schools and the Charlotte-Mecklenburg Schools. Lynn was my mentor, during my nontenured years, as a novice math teacher in Charlotte. She visited and observed my classroom and had a way of developing professional and personal relationships with new teachers by asking them to self-reflect and celebrate success. I did not realize that she was modeling for me the skills and qualities of how to be a great leader.

I completed a master's degree in school administration at Cambridge College and then became the math facilitator at James Martin Middle School. This was my first instructional leadership role outside of the classroom. My strategic plans assisted our school to make high growth in mathematics for the first time in five years under the leadership of Dr. Anne Renfro. Two years later, I accepted the position as the assistant principal at Pasquotank County High School in the Elizabeth City–Pasquotank Public Schools in North Carolina. Truly, nothing could have prepared me for my first year as administrator, but once I was in the assistant principal role, I discovered that Lynn's notes, books, professional learning communities, and many of her professional development sessions on building leaders helped me to follow and lead in a new learning environment.

Chapter 3, Building Relationships, is the most significant for me, because it details how to bring together all stakeholders in a learning community to increase student achievement. I created a school culture at Pasquotank County High School that increased student performance. Three years later, I believed that I was ready to take the lead and accepted the role as the principal at Bertie STEM High School in Windsor, North Carolina.

I accepted the district's highest honor as the principal of the year and completed the National Association of Elementary School Principals (NAESP) Principal Mentor Program, both in 2013.

I find myself not able to read *Supporting New Teachers: A How-To Guide for Leaders* continuously. I discovered that each chapter must be consumed like a mini chocolate. Eat a few chapters at time, to savor the taste and enjoy moments of opportunities to grow and learn as an educational leader.

—Lisa Parker
Principal of the Year, Bertie County Schools, NC

Preface

I really love to travel, both for work and pleasure. It has always been an adventure to navigate the airlines, the roads, and the extraneous things that just get in the way. I served on a national speakers' bureau for six years and traveled around the United States and Canada doing professional development for science education. It was a wonderful experience to meet educators from kindergarten to college level. I had been invited to speak in Seattle and meet with the National Geoscience Teacher's Board, so I decided to go out a few days early to visit Mt. St. Helens. My husband and I had been in there in 1985, and I wanted to see the difference that 10 years had made in the environmental recovery of the area. I drove the three hours from Seattle and took the 21-mile, winding road up to the summit. However, in late October, freezing fog was moving into the area, and visibility was reduced to zero. There had been no other cars on the road, no live or dead animals, and nothing but cold rain and fog. I parked the car next to a sign pointing to Mt. St. Helens and took a picture to document that I had been there. I decided to stop at a turnout and use one of the port-a-potties before my return to Seattle. I walked in, closed the door and heard a click. There was a small lock on the outside which engaged upon my shutting the door. I was locked in a port-a-potty and 21 miles from nowhere!

I tell this story because it is a great analogy for what we often do to new teachers. The fact that this situation happened to involve a modern convenience is not the issue. This event made me afraid and insecure, and I felt a need for survival. Although your new teachers are not physically locked in an outhouse, the feeling I had there relates to the fear, loneliness, and sense of total helplessness of being in a classroom on the first day of school. Not having the necessary skills and knowledge needed to survive puts new teachers at a tremendous disadvantage during their first year.

A VISION OF TEACHING

I think about my first year of teaching and wonder how it was similar to or different from the first years of so many educators of the past. As a child, I watched my mother and stepgrandmother deal with the daily issues of teaching and their constant attention to grading and planning for the next day. It was clear to me that I would never, ever want to teach school. I can clearly remember telling my mother that under no circumstances would I become a teacher, as I saw that she truly had no life except for middle school English. I wanted to be a pathologist, because dead people don't talk back and aren't disrespectful or unruly. After working in a juvenile delinquency center in Atlanta, my mind was changed for good, and I did go into education, because I knew that I could make a difference. My first day of teaching was an incredible, yet horrific, experience. I just didn't realize how unprepared I was for the first 24 hours and the first year. I found that the support from my principal was limited, and my colleagues liked to stay in their rooms and not communicate or collaborate.

LOOKING THROUGH THE EYES OF A NEW TEACHER

This book is for leaders who want to help their new educators survive and develop into effective, exemplary teachers. I have a passion for new teachers, and you may never meet anyone with such a desire to save and support each of them as they work toward a rewarding career in education. My first day of teaching was not a perfect day. After student teaching in advanced placement biology and chemistry, the only job I could get was an eighth-grade earth science position at the junior high. I clearly remember the 187 students who came into a classroom with no desks or books and a brand new teacher with no content knowledge or skills with this age group. And the teacher next door who reminded me how many days I had until retirement and the fact that I was "given" the varsity and junior varsity cheerleaders to coach, and having no clue what to do with them. I began to question my career choice on the evening our bus was assaulted by the opposing players, who threw rocks and bottles at us after losing to our basketball team. Had it not been for the fact that I was not a quitter and really needed a job, I would probably have left teaching, because I had absolutely no support. What you do in your district or school will make the difference in building capacity for retaining and creating quality educators for your students.

As I write this book, I look through the eyes of a new teacher and remember how hard it really was those first several years. My experiences have taken me into many schools in rural, suburban, and urban areas of the country. I have been in classrooms that are running like clockwork, with engagement, motivation, and evidence of high expectations that all students will achieve. I have also been in classrooms where there is an obvious lack of support from the administration, and where there are management and organizational problems and student indifference. Would you want to be a new teacher today? This question is always answered with mixed results from veteran educators. With the endless issues facing our teachers today, the answer is often a "no," and I always want to know why. Recently, I asked a group of 50 seasoned K–12 teachers to give me a list of things they wished they had known prior to their first day in the classroom. Their answers included lesson design, classroom management, logistics of the school, grades, paychecks, and substitutes, and the list went on and on. As administrators, we need to step back from our administrative roles and remember what it was like to be a new teacher. Put yourself back into that first day in the classroom, and ask yourself what you needed and whether it was provided.

I want you to consider how best to use the strategies and ideas in the book. As you read through the text, think about these suggestions:

- Pick a topic, and read through that specific chapter to learn new ideas.

- Select a set of self-reflection questions, and take time to think about your responses along with your current successes and challenges.

- Think about the process that you have in place for new teacher support. What can you continue to do, and what can you improve so that your new teachers can be successful?

- Read through the scenarios, and relate to these actual situations. Do you have a similar experience that you can correlate to your own position?

- Decide what the most current needs are for your new teachers, and find strategies and suggestions to support their improvement.

- Think about how you are building leadership capacity within your building and how to involve your new staff in sharing their experiences and growth for learning.

Acknowledgments

When you think about who to thank for your success, the list is long. Thanks to my family, friends, new teachers, and leaders for their support and guidance in completing another book. I appreciate their wisdom and knowledge that provided the stories and experiences for the book. There are several people, however, who have made the difference, and I want to thank them personally.

- Wallace, my husband, who after 40 years understands my need to be busy and challenged. As a former kindergarten teacher, he taught me that if it doesn't work in kindergarten, it just doesn't work.

- My Mom and Dad who gave me independence, a sense of value, and the desire to be an individual with a mission in life.

- Elizabeth and Linda, my best friends, who often tell me that I just fell off the earth but continued to be there when I needed them.

- Catherine, my former student, family member, and colleague, for giving me stories and the motivation to continue in my quest to support new teachers.

- Calvin Wallace, my former boss and friend, who hired me because I told him the truth and was a bit snippy. He taught me more in five years than I learned from all of the other years in education combined. He allowed me to do what I do best, and that was to improve instruction in our Region B schools in the Charlotte-Mecklenburg Schools. His respect, rapport, and wisdom will never be forgotten by me or anyone that ever had the opportunity to work with him.

- McKinley Johnson and every other new teacher that has shared stories and anecdotes with me. Thank you for your dedication and commitment to staying with it and making a difference in the lives of young people every day.

- Jack Baldermann, principal at Westmont High School, for truly turning a school around. His compassion and love of learning changed the way his staff and students met goals and achieved.

- Dr. Lynnice Carter, assistant superintendent in Pontotoc County Schools, Mississippi, for her dedication to making learning relevant and applicable for her new teachers.

- Rob Clark, principal, Jennifer Moore, assistant principal, and Paula Jones, mentor, at William Blount High School in Maryville, Tennessee, who just get excited about their role in helping new teachers transition from the business world to be effective educators.

- Debra Gladstone, principal at Mineral Springs Elementary, for her enthusiasm and excitement about being an administrator and the role she plays in supporting her school community.

- Ynez Olshausen, principal at Waddell Language Academy, for being a friend and colleague for the past 15 years, and for her undying efforts to create a unique, global language-learning school.

- Lisa Parker, lateral entry first-year teacher, assistant principal, principal, central office administrator, and curriculum/instructional specialist for Bertie County Schools in Windsor, North Carolina, for her love of education. Thank you for the opportunity to serve as a mentor.

- Chris Pearson, principal at West View Elementary School in the Burlington-Edison School District in Washington, for his commitment to collaboration, visibility, and decision sharing.

- Jay Posick, principal at Merton Intermediate School in Merton, Wisconsin, for his enthusiasm and dedication to building positive relationships with his staff, students, and school community.

- Dr. Lena Marie Rockwood, assistant principal at Rumney Marsh Academy in the Revere Public Schools in Massachusetts, for her passion and positive feedback and her role in making her school look good.

PUBLISHER'S ACKNOWLEDGMENTS

Corwin gratefully acknowledges the contributions of the following reviewers:

Lydia Adegbola
Assistant Principal
New York City Department
   of Education
New York, NY

Sean Beggin
Assistant Principal
Anoka Hennepin Secondary
   Technical Education Program
Anoka, MN

Dr. LaQuita Outlaw
Principal
Bay Shore Middle School
Bay Shore, NY

Lena Marie Rockwood
Middle School Assistant Principal
Rumney Marsh Academy
Revere, MA

About the Author

 **Lynn F. Howard** is an author, professional development associate, and teacher. She has worked for the Leadership and Learning Center for the past 10 years and in the Charlotte-Mecklenburg School System for more than 30 years as a middle-grades science and math teacher, coordinator of the gifted program, and K–12 regional assistant superintendent for curriculum and instruction. She served on the speakers' bureau of the National Association of Geoscience Education as a keynoter, board member, and professional developer.

Lynn has presented at state and regional conferences of the Association of Supervision and Curriculum Development, the National Science Teachers Association, Phi Delta Kappa, Learning Forward, the International Reading Association, and the Association for Middle Level Educators.

She has published numerous books, including *Ready for Anything: Supporting New Teachers for Success* (2006), and three versions of *Five Easy Steps to a Balanced Science Program* (2010) for different grade levels. She wrote "Connecting Science Standards and Assessments," a chapter in *Standards and Assessment: The Core of Quality Instruction* (Lead + Learn Press, 2011). Her latest chapters, "Success in the Beginning: Supporting New Teachers" and "Balanced Science Instruction" are published in *Engaged Instruction: Thriving Classroom in the Age of the Common Core* (Lead + Learn Press, 2014). Lynn also contributed to the new *Response to Instructional Strategies and Interventions: Scenarios for K–12 Educators* by Dr. Linda Gregg (Lead + Learn Press, 2012)

Lynn holds a master's degree in earth science and education and a bachelor's degree in biology from the University of North Carolina at Charlotte, academy certification from the National Staff Development Council, and national certification in gifted and talented education.

Introduction

Teacher retention and recruitment is not new and will continue to be a national issue. About a quarter of entering public school teachers leave teaching within the first three years (U.S. Department of Education, 2007). In schools with low academic achievement, the rates are higher, suggesting that programs to reduce teacher attrition may be needed to improve teaching and learning. In a blog post entitled "The Teacher Dropout Crisis," Aly Seidel (2014) discussed a report from the Alliance for Excellent Education that indicated that "roughly half a million U.S. teachers either move or leave the profession each year." And, the study said, at-risk students suffer the most from the loss of these teachers. High turnover creates instability in schools, making it more difficult to have a coherent school community. With an influx of new teachers each year, repeat training and support promotes inconsistency rather than a continual improvement process. In addition, the attrition rate of first-year teachers has increased by about one third in the past two decades. This mean that there are far more beginning educators, but they are less likely to stay in teaching.

I often ask principals whether it is better to recruit or retain teachers. Overall, the response is to retain them and have them want to come back for another year. In 1988, there were about 65,000 first-year teachers, and the most common teacher was a veteran with 15 years of teaching experience. By 2008, the number of first-year teachers has increased to more than 200,000. In 2013, there were more than 3 million full-time teachers according to the Department of Education. Nearly 20% of teachers at high-poverty schools leave each year, which is a rate 50% higher than at more affluent schools. That equates to one of every five teachers leaving by the next year. In high-turnover schools, students may be more likely to have inexperienced teachers who we know are less effective on average than experienced teachers (Rockoff, 2004).

Teachers are more educated than ever before, with the proportion of those holding master's degrees increasing to 50% from 23% since the early 1960s. Only 6% of teachers are African American; 5% are Hispanic or Asian or come from other ethnic groups. Men represent barely a quarter of teachers; this is the lowest level in four decades.

We also know that comprehensive induction and new teacher support programs have made a difference for many new educators. States spend millions of dollars each year to replace teachers who have left the profession rather than investing in implementing a process that supports teachers' learning. In both small and large districts around the country, a study by the National Commission on Teaching and America's Future (2007) found that the costs of recruiting, hiring, and training a replacement teacher can be substantial. In Granville County, North Carolina, the cost of replacing each teacher who left the district was just under $10,000. In Jemez Valley, New Mexico, a small rural district, the cost per teacher leaving is $4,366. In Milwaukee, Wisconsin, the average cost per teacher leaver was $15,325. In a very large district like that in Chicago, the average cost was $17,872 per leaver. The total cost of turnover in the Chicago Public Schools is estimated to be more than $86 million per year.

Over the last 20 years, the importance of teacher induction has gained support within the 50 states. The proportion of new teachers receiving induction support rose from 41% in 1990 to almost 75% in 2008 (National Comprehensive Center for Teacher Quality, 2010).

WHY TEACHERS QUIT

Surveys completed by first-year teachers identify a variety of factors that contribute to their leaving or their willingness to stay and continue. One of the most common reasons teachers leave is lack of support from the administration, specifically the principal. Principals who make a concerted effort to create conditions that support and nurture new staff have greater teacher retention. Many teachers remark that although tangible items are very useful in the classroom, it is personal interaction and communication with the principal that make the ultimate difference in their decision to return to or leave a particular school.

New teachers usually find that they are unprepared for the reality of the classroom. In addition to not having building principal support, surveys found the following as factors for teachers leaving:

- Not feeling valued

- Feeling isolated and alone with their problems and without access to someone to help them

- Too much paperwork, lack of planning time, and not enough time in general

- Student behavior

- Lack of knowledge about the required duties and assignments within their grade level and school

- Inadequate salary and benefits

- Relocation and family commitment

While teacher retention is addressed, the goal may not be to achieve zero turnover rates. There are many factors involved in teachers leaving, including personal reasons, such as relocation or retirement, that are not controlled by the district or school. Some new teachers may also find that teaching is just not for them and that they are better off making the choice to leave. The need to have a well-managed system of support, including entrance and exit surveys, is paramount in staffing schools.

NEW TEACHER SUPPORT PROGRAMS

Districts around the country refer to new teachers with a variety of terms: *beginning, lateral entry, inexperienced, rookie,* and *novice.* This book uses many of these terms interchangeably, and how you describe your new educators will depend on the vocabulary of your area. For our purposes, a *new* or *beginning* teacher may be one who

- has no prior background or experience.
- may have certification and college coursework but has just been hired.
- has experience but is moving into a new district or school.

Induction and new teacher support programs are the activities and strategies used to grow a novice teacher into the status of proficient educator. These programs include orientation, professional development, mentoring, and peer support groups. Over the past 20 years, the number and type of induction programs have increased steadily. In 1990, 50% of new teachers stated that they participated in some kind of induction program, while in 2008, 91% had been involved in some kind of support program during their first year of teaching. Twenty-seven states require some kind of induction program for new teachers (Goldrick, Osta, Barlin, & Burn, 2012).

While the number of induction programs has increased, the kind of support that states, districts, and schools provide varies. The most common is regular supportive communication from the principal or other administrators. Some say that they receive ongoing support from a mentor teacher. Collaboration and planning with other teachers was also high on the list.

However, it is the level and quality of implementation that makes all of this work. Numbers and data speak loudly to retention and attrition rates for new teachers, but it is what happens within the school walls that will truly make a difference.

In the 2012–13 MetLife "Survey of the American Teacher" (MetLife, 2013), new teachers reported being greatly stressed by administrative duties, classroom management, and testing responsibilities as well as by their relationships (or lack thereof) with their students' parents. Although some of the reasons are beyond our control, we should ask ourselves what we can control and how we can resolve the issues. Recognizing and understanding the barriers should be the integral focus of a strong induction program. Analyzing and implementing an action plan is an obligation and an opportunity to make a difference in new teacher support.

Teachers with fewer than five years of experience provided me a list of items that they felt would have been beneficial in their retention. They suggested the following:

- Daily time to interact with their mentor or other highly qualified educators in their building and on their grade level.

- A mentor who was nonjudgmental, provided constructive feedback, and cared about them professionally and personally.

- Someone who checked on them every day and asked what they needed both tangibly and emotionally.

- Detailed information about the expectations at their school, specifically from the administrative staff. This included goals, behavior policies, standards and lesson planning, and community relationships.

- A monthly (or more frequent) support group where they could meet with other first-year teachers and their mentors to discuss like issues and concerns. This was specifically a time to vent and learn how to deal with the daily issues of teaching.

Before beginning or supplementing a new teacher support process, take time to review the following guiding questions and reflect on current practices.

- What are you doing well?
- Do you have a new teacher support program in place at your school?
- Who is conducting new teacher professional development in your school?
- Where can you make improvements?
- Do teachers want to stay at or leave your school?
- How have you implemented your own personal action growth plan?

RATIONALE FOR SUPPORTING NEW TEACHERS

Teachers make a difference in the lives of students every day. The impact that one teacher has on a student is immeasurable in relationship building, student achievement, and lifelong skills for learning. If we recognize that teacher quality is the greatest predictor of student success, we see that the need to develop and implement a well-designed support program could not be more critical.

All of us should have a goal of retaining effective teachers and having them want to return to education year after year. The ownership of teacher retention should be a concerted effort at the school level through a continuous, well-designed flow of professional development and support targeted at the skill and knowledge development of new teachers. Our new staff must have close access to support from the building principal, mentors, and colleagues who can provide their expertise in curriculum design, classroom management, and instructional delivery. Schools should develop a plan that will

- provide sustained professional development that is relevant and aligned with teachers' needs.

- model, apply, and allow for implementation of classroom management and instructional strategies.

- allow for administrative support, specifically from the building principal.

- improve the level of teacher satisfaction.

- raise student achievement through teacher capacity building.

HOW TO USE THE BOOK

I wrote this book to help with new teacher support. It is designed for all administrators, including principals, assistant principals, coaches, mentors, lead teachers, and other school leaders who want to make a difference. With public education in the national news, it is imperative that we take ownership of how we change the way we support and develop our teachers so that our students are the winners. New teachers are our link to improving teaching and learning, and with so many coming into the profession, we cannot ignore the fact that we are clearly in charge of their success. The question is, what are you doing to retain and build capacity with your new staff members?

This book presents the actions and strategies needed for administrative leaders to take charge of what happens with new teacher induction and support. There are both *what to do* and *how to do it* ideas and suggestions based on real-world school scenarios. Everything in the book is based on best practices from leadership and teaching and years of experience as a teacher, instructional leader, mentor, and professional developer. It is also based on stories and anecdotes from hundreds of conversations with educators around the country.

It does not contain every possible strategy, method, or suggestion for new teachers' success, but it presents ideas that administrators can use and implement. It does not guarantee 100% retention, but it does provide strategies for improving new teacher support.

I will hope that everyone reading the book has some remembrance of being a first-year teacher and how hard it was to overcome all of the obstacles. If you reflect back on your first year and think of all the things you wished you had known prior to the first day, you will be able to empathize with the need for support and guidance that your new staff deserves.

I hope that you will find something that you can use in your school to help with building capacity for teaching and learning. If it just takes some small tweaks in what you already have, then have fun with some new strategies and ideas. Whatever the case, just do something that you can be proud of and call your own. After all, you are the instructional leader for all around you.

It is my intention to have this book validate some of the things you are already doing in your building and also to provide you with some additional ideas and suggestions. You must decide where your most urgent needs are with your new staff, challenge your current practices, and create an action plan that is personal to you as an instructional leader.

It will take some effort and time on your part to focus on what is needed in your building. Your job as an administrator is not easy, and balancing the day-to-day routines will be difficult, but the final decision of building a school culture that improves teaching and learning is up to you.

HOW THE BOOK IS ORGANIZED

This book is simple to use. Each chapter includes five common points. These will help you organize your thoughts and actions as you begin to develop a plan for new teacher support. The purpose is to provide you with simple and easy-to-use strategies, suggestions, and reflections that will improve teacher effectiveness in your school. Logistical ideas and strategies that administrators can implement are included in each chapter. Personal stories from the field, related to the needs of new teachers, are included to reinforce the strategies presented in each section. Please feel free to reflect on each and relate it to your own experiences. You may find that you won't read the book in order, but rather pick out a strategy related to your need.

Quotes That Support the Work

When I was in college, I took a course in literature and found that the professor began each day with a quote related to the topic of the morning. At first, I really did not understand the purpose of this, especially since I was a math and science major, but I came to realize the importance that each quote had for my learning. The quotes are designed for you to use to reflect and share your experiences with others. Many of my instructional leaders use these on staff and parent newsletters, as an opening discussion starter at meetings, and as a reflective part of professional learning team time.

Stories From the Field

My work in education has taken me to many school districts, schools, and individual classrooms. From the moment you walk into a school building to the time you walk out, there are always stories of educators doing the right, and sometimes wrong, things in teaching. The stories are intended to support your thoughts about new teachers. All of them are true and reflect the learning experiences that made new teachers into great educators. As the instructional leader, please use these stories or some of your own to share your background and personal anecdotes with your new teachers. This will help you build positive relationships.

The Administrator's Role

This section provides background and information that support the suggested strategies found in the book along with current trends and research-based practices. The book presents ideas for implementing a new teacher support process or improving an existing school-based program.

If we recognize that teacher quality is the greatest predictor of student success, we understand the need to develop, implement, and monitor a well-designed series of support processes within our building.

What Else Can I Do?

This section provides specific ideas and suggestions that leaders can use within their own building to help new teachers be successful. These are content-generic, are appropriate for all grade levels, require little time for preparation, and are based on research into best practices. In some cases, checklists and implementation worksheets are provided to help guide your action planning. Multiple templates are included to help in your discussions and support processes.

Self-Reflection Questions

John Hattie, in *Visible Learning* (2009), wrote that he found that students who reflect on their work and anticipate their scores have greater achievement levels. While his findings were related to students, it is important to note that adults can also effectively estimate their own performance and level of achievement. There is power in setting goals, enhancing learning, and gaining confidence in trying new opportunities. I encourage not only you but also your new teachers to reflect and assess each day on the successes and challenges. The self-reflection section has questions related to the specific topic and will allow you to think about the impact you are making as you move through the year. You should be able to chart your journey as the instructional leader for your new teachers and identify your strengths and areas for improvement.

1

Instructional Leadership

QUOTE

I love problem solving and puzzles. I love to find solutions and my goal is to make all teachers successful. I have learned that leadership emerges when things are going badly. Powerful lessons are learned by making inadvertent mistakes. It is not just a job—it goes beyond that. It is getting people to know how we do things here and creating a culture that is purposeful and task-oriented.

—Ynez Olshausen, principal

STORY FROM THE FIELD

Ynez Olshausen is the principal at Waddell Language Academy. She has been an administrator for 26 years, having begun her career at the Department of Defense. Her school is a public K–8 magnet in the Charlotte-Mecklenburg School District, and offers students the opportunity to become fluent and literate in a second language. Waddell Language Academy offers second language immersion instruction in Chinese, German, French, and Japanese. Ynez's staff is unique in that they represent a diverse number of cultures and experiences, many of which are not common in American schools. They have the skills, motivation, and desire to be exemplary educators, but they often do not know how American schools operate. Ynez continuously asks herself: "What else do I need to teach them, and how do I find out what they need to know and share with them in a nonblaming way?" She addresses terminology and vocabulary, dress codes, grading, and parent communications on a regular basis. One of her teachers told a parent that the child was "lazy," a term used in the teacher's native country. Ynez had to talk with the teacher about using appropriate language terms so that the teacher could continue to build positive relationships with the students and parents.

THE ADMINISTRATOR'S ROLE

It has been said over and over that the building principal has the largest impact on new teacher retention and job satisfaction. What you do in the beginning will determine what happens over the span of a school year. New teacher programs have been implemented across the country with great success in some areas and no success in others. Many school districts are still providing "rookie camp" during the professional development days before school starts. New educators gather in a large arena, and people come in and talk at them about all aspects of their new teaching career. Other districts provide monthly seminars or mentors so that support can be ongoing throughout the year. In some cases, districts provide a book that addresses what the new teacher can do to build the skills and knowledge needed for a successful teaching career. There are a lot of pages with suggestions and strategies, but my experience has shown that most new teachers really don't have the time to read them.

While these books are excellent sources of information, they do not provide the practical application and support that new teachers need. Nor do they support administrators with information about what their role is in new teacher support. The problem with these books is that they provide too much information, while administrators provide no modeling or demonstration of the practices by the instructional leader of the school. New teachers want to see a strategy demonstrated, practice it, and then get feedback on how they are doing.

The Importance of the Building Principal

My principal is totally with it and really cares about me. Instead of asking me "How are you doing?" she asks me "What can I do for you today?" If she asked me the first question, I would tell her "fine," which is really not the case at all. She walks the hall every morning and makes an effort to speak to all of us. I see that she has a small notepad with her and writes down a to-do list for each of us. If she were not present, I would not feel as good about being here as I do.

—Elizabeth, K–8 media specialist

John Hattie, in *Visible Learning* (2009), wrote about his extensive research into and synthesis of 800 meta-analyses on what works in schools, and he has provided educators with the research data needed to significantly impact teaching and learning. Hattie's work presents research involving millions of students and represents the largest compilation of evidence-based research into the multiple influences that affect student achievement.

A report by the Public Education Network in 2003 clearly found the importance of the principal's role in making a first-year teacher successful. The report shows that new teachers who stated their schools were run by principals they described as *effective* and *competent* had an easier transition into teaching. At the top of their list was the attribute of being *accessible*. A principal who had time to meet with new teachers, so they could ask questions and discuss successes and challenges, was a critical component of effective new teacher support models.

The building principal's role has changed over the past few years. A study from the Wallace Foundation in 2010 found that principals are second only to teachers in the impact made on student achievement and overall school success. Effective leaders work on being effective, and it takes time and effort.

This study suggests that effective leadership encompasses five key responsibilities:

- Shaping a vision of academic success for all students, one based on high standards.

- Creating a climate hospitable to education so that safety, a cooperative spirit, and other foundations of fruitful interaction prevail.

- Cultivating leadership in others so that teachers and other adults assume their part in realizing the school vision.

- Improving instruction to enable teachers to teach at their best and students to learn at their utmost.

- Managing people, data, and processes to foster school improvement.

What Kind of Leader Are You?

John Hattie (2009) discussed two types of leadership: instructional and transformational. He stated,

> Instructional leadership refers to those principals who have their major focus on creating a learning climate free of disruption, a system of clear teaching objectives, and high teacher expectations for teachers and students. Transformational leadership refers to those principals who engage with their teaching staff in ways that inspire them to new levels of energy, commitment, and moral purpose. The evidence from the meta-analyses supports the power of the former over the latter in terms of the effects on students' outcomes.

It is school leaders who promote challenging goals then establish safe environments for teachers to critique, question, and support other teachers to reach these goals together that have most effect on student outcomes. (p. 83)

When you talk with Ynez Olshausen at Waddell Language Academy, you get the sense of her leadership style after several minutes of conversation. She is well versed in current research on effective schools, instructional best practices, and leadership skills. Her expectations are fair and consistent across the K–8 grade levels, and she recognizes that challenge is part of all district and school programs and initiatives. She is very good at sharing current data and information—not perceptions—from the national, state, and local agencies so that her teachers are well informed on what is happening in educational trends. Her philosophy is that the school is not a "have it your way" school but one that is built on communication that supports shared decision-making that is in the best interest of everyone in the building.

Lessons Learned About Leadership

The heart of school improvement is in improving daily teaching and learning practices, balanced with the appropriate level of evaluation, including daily collaborating at the school setting. School leaders are responsible for cultural changes, and what they do with modeling practices and behaviors makes an impact on teaching and learning. Permeating the cultures of effective schools were nine principles that I found to establish positive communities for teaching and learning. When I interviewed leaders around the country, I found that each one of these was in the forefront of their leadership styles and practices.

Ask yourself how you implement and model these principles in your daily connections within your school community. Write down your reflections as you read through the actions, and choose several in which to improve throughout the year.

1. Model and implement high expectations for all.

All of us in education believe that all children can learn. It is written on mission and vision statements across the country, and we have spent countless hours helping our school communities understand that this is truly what we see as our goal in education.

- Determine your expectations for teaching, management, and behavior in your building.

- Post your mission and vision statement within the school, and refer to it often.

- Have grade levels and/or individual classrooms establish their own mission and vision statements, and refer to them often.

- Start the school year with high expectations. Define what excellent teaching will be in your school, and establish a set of goals for making the environment a better place for teaching and learning.

- Meet with your new teachers, individually, to talk about implementing their goals.

- Establish the fact that you are a support for your teachers.

2. Develop and maintain strong interpersonal connections between students and adults.

The adults in the building are your strongest resource, and what happens between classroom teachers and their students will impact the success of your school. Teachers have to like the students they are teaching. Building relationships is one of the most important aspects of effective teaching.

- Frequently recognize excellence in your new staff.

- Congratulate your staff members when they do exceptional work in the classroom.

- Recognize new teacher milestones during the year.

- Talk to your new teachers about staying for the next year. You should begin these conversations around the middle of November. Explain why you need them and need them to stay.

- Start every staff meeting or e-mail with a thank you and note of appreciation.

- Cover a class if there is an emergency. Sometimes substitutes are hard to find at the last moment.

3. Focus on student engagement and motivation in all classrooms.

Students should be engaged with learning, and teachers should be motivated to come to school.

Several years ago, I was interviewed by a local TV news crew about teacher morale and motivation. The anchorwoman asked me a variety of questions about what makes effective schools and how teacher retention impacted student learning. One of her questions struck me as really strange. She asked me, "What motivates you to come to school?" I did not have to think about the answer and replied very quickly, "If I have to motivate myself, then who will motivate my students?"

- Define what engagement means to you, your teachers, and your students.

- Talk about motivation and the impact it has on teaching and learning. Find out what motivates your new staff to come to work every day.

- Ask your students: "What are you learning today?" You should not accept comments such as "nothing," "I don't know," or "math." There should be a specific, standard-based response that indicates the teacher has shared the learning outcomes for the day.

- Find out what strategies the teacher has tried with the students. Talk about building relationships and getting to know the students.

4. Implement a rich and engaging curriculum, including standards and assessments.

The new Common Core State Standards for English Language Arts and Mathematics and the Next Generation Science Standards have once again changed the way we approach curriculum in this country. Whether you have adopted these is not important, but having a strategy that integrates best practices for curriculum design is critical to improving student achievement in your school.

- Share your expertise about the curriculum with your teachers. What are the skills and content that students must be able to do and know in order to be successful?

- Provide a systematic method to "tame the standards" using a curriculum design process for writing rigorous units of study by grade level and content area.

- Discuss the informal components of the school day, such as social, emotional, and physical learning activities.

- Provide opportunities for teachers to learn what the standards are saying and what they mean in terms of implementation

5. Implement and monitor effective teaching practices in all classrooms on a daily basis.

Marzano, Pickering, and Pollock's *Classroom Instruction That Works* (2001) and John Hattie's *Visible Learning* (2009) clearly define the best instructional practices that make a difference in schools.

- Conduct a book study of best instructional practices focusing on one or two each month during a staff meeting.

- Allow your new teachers to observer master teachers, either in your building or at a colleague's site.

- Use videos to show model classrooms. These are readily available on the Internet for all content areas and grade levels. Many offer discussion questions to guide the viewing.

- Model best practices at staff meetings to show that you are aware of current research-based strategies that work.

- Hold a round table discussion at a staff meeting. Place selected best practices on index cards, and have teachers share how to actually use these in the classroom.

- Explain the importance of the Standards for Mathematical Practice for Common Core Math, the Practices for Common Core English/Language Arts, and the Science and Engineering Practices in the Next Generation Science Standards. Using chart paper, have teachers find the key points and the implications for instruction and assessment.

6. Provide data analysis and feedback to ensure teacher and student improvement.

The responsibility for data analysis and feedback is one of your most important jobs in the building. You have a lot of numbers to crunch and must decide how to share the most important data with your staff. Data sources inform and guide actions, and without meaningful data, you will not know the effectiveness of your initiatives. Your role is to constantly review, refine, and realign practices that reflect specific needs based on data analysis.

- Decide which data are the most critical to use to inform your decisions. For example, this could include behavior, attendance, assessment, or other related data points.

- Design your learning community teams so that there is uninterrupted time to collaborate and share information.

- Establish goals for student achievement that are specific, relevant, timely, and measurable. For example, improving algebra scores from 33% to 45% proficient is more realistic than setting a goal of 100% proficiency over a span of 6 weeks.

- Determine the type of feedback that will make a difference in teacher actions.

7. Learn what to say and what not to say.

All of us have said things that we regret or have said something in the wrong way or format. A group of teachers recently shared with me comments that they had heard their principal say during the year. These statements reflect the culture that is established in the building. Decide where the culture of your organization falls within these two sections.

- Here are a few things to say that will make a difference in teacher morale and illustrate that you are taking an interest in your new staff.
  - "I appreciate you."
  - "What do you need?" or "How can I make your job easier?" or "How are you doing for materials and supplies?"
  - "You handled that situation very well."

   ○ "I respect you and your dedication to our students."

   ○ "Thank you for letting me know. I will investigate your concern and get back to you with more information."

   ○ "I want your input on something. Can we find a time to chat?"

   ○ "Thank you for being confidential on this matter. Trust me to follow through."

   ○ "We work for our students and school community."

   ○ "Do you mind if I share this success at the staff meeting tomorrow?"

- Here are a few things to never, ever say out loud.

   ○ "How are you doing?" because the response will be "Fine."

   ○ "Before I make a decision, I want to hear the student's version." You just need to rephrase this one, so is doesn't sound like you doubt your teacher's judgment.

   ○ "If you could only handle your classroom . . ."

   ○ "Put it in my box and I will get to it."

   ○ "I don't know what to do about that."

   ○ "We have a difficult group of students, parents, situations . . ."

   ○ "Don't you know where these kids come from?"

8. Minimize disruptions for teachers and students. Allow teaching and learning to occur.

I was recently in a middle school where it seemed that the priority was on interrupting the instructional day as often as possible. Announcements, class change bells, people coming and going from classrooms, custodial cleaning, bathroom breaks, students wandering the halls, and fire drills were destroying every teaching moment possible. New teachers are often thrown off course in their lesson implementation when the class period is constantly in disarray. These interruptions waste time that could be used for instructional learning and can also lead to behavioral problems for students.

- Decide on when whole school announcements will be made during the day.

- Pull students out of class only when necessary.

- Make sure teachers have consistent schedules for lunch, recess, and restroom breaks.

- Establish a respectful noise level for the halls and for transitioning time between classes.

- Establish a schoolwide hall pass or escort policy.

- Walk your halls and identify students out of place. Take action when you see something.

9. Develop strong positive relationships within your school community.

Your actions and your new teachers' relationships within the school community are important in establishing good working conditions for all stakeholders.

- Keep your communications short and to the point. People will read about 30 seconds of what you send home.

- Do not use acronyms. Most people don't know what they stand for.

- Do your job, and do it effectively.

- Have a school community communication plan. Base this on your audience; you will need to create differentiated methods for communicating with your parents and students. This may include writing information in different languages, establishing a consistent time for newsletters or e-mails, and scheduling school-based activities at times and locations that are convenient for your diverse community.

- Quickly dispel misconceptions or rumors. In a crisis, communicate the facts as quickly as possible—using all media sources—to staff, parents, and students.

- Communicate face-to-face as often as possible. Use focus groups, phone trees, blogs, and e-mail. Walk the halls and talk to people.

- Tell families, if applicable, that they can get into district athletic events with no charge. This helps them connect to what their students are doing outside of class and at no cost to them.

Ynez will tell you that "leadership emerges when things are going badly," and effective leaders make decisions that include showing confidence, modeling expectations, and inspiring others to do the same. I have often heard her tell people that she uses the Swiss watch as an analogy for making her school work. Every piece has to be in place, and all pieces have to work together for the 1,400 students in her building. She adds that a fair and consistent plan to get from point A to point B must be well executed on a minute-to-minute basis. When challenges get in the way, you deal with them in an equitable fashion and move on to the next thing. The way the staff and students present themselves to others is what they are all about and it sends the message that school and learning is important to all.

WHAT ELSE CAN I DO?

Several principals suggested that leaders have a Principal's To-Do List (Figure 1.1) as they develop an action plan for supporting their new staff members. With the changing role of administrators, it is easy to forget or put to the side the things that we need to accomplish on a daily basis that show the support and guidance that is needed to create great teachers.

Take a moment and use the list to focus on one or two priority areas that will support your new staff members. Write down your thoughts as an action plan.

Figure 1.1 Principal's To-Do List

Focusing on School Climate	My Strategies
Defining high expectations • Academic • Behavior • Attendance • Instruction • Assessment • Communication	
Modeling respect, confidence, and trust	
Encouraging collegiality and effective teaming	
Promoting risk taking and experimentation	
Providing honest, open communication	
Honoring traditions and individual cultures	

Focusing on School Climate	My Strategies
Modeling appreciation, celebration, and recognition of all school community members	
Promoting the vision and mission	
Using teachers' and community members' strengths	
Including everyone in the decision-making process	
Supporting professionalism in all areas	
Monitoring engagement and motivation in the classrooms	

SELF-REFLECTION QUESTIONS

Take time to reflect on the questions in Figure 1.2 related to your role as a leader and your support of your new teachers. Your responses in both the strengths and challenges columns should help guide you with implementing strategies that will impact your school community. You should be able to chart your journey as the instructional leader as you progress through the year.

Figure 1.2 Self-Reflection Questions

Reflection Questions	My Strengths	My Challenges	My Strategies
How do I let my teachers know that I am part of their instructional team?			
How do I practice effective listening skills?			
How do I pick my battles and evaluate all sides in a situation before making a decision?			
In what way do I have an open-door policy and meet with my new teachers at least once a month?			
Do I remember being a teacher?			
What people connections do I make every day?			

Reflection Questions	My Strengths	My Challenges	My Strategies
Which is better: identifying problems or identifying solutions? Why?			
How do I value everyone in my school community?			
How often do I say "thank you"?			
How do I design quality professional development based on my staff's needs?			
What opportunities do I provide so my staff can attend professional development at local, state, and national conferences?			
How accessible am I to my staff?			
How visible am I on a daily basis?			
How do I let my new teachers know that they are special by providing small goodies and notes of appreciation for them?			

2

Planning for New Teacher Support

QUOTE

I often think I might get a speeding ticket on my way to school. I just can't wait to start a new day. We don't start until 8:45 but I am always here at 6:30 and ready to make a difference with my staff and students.

—Debra Gladstone, principal

STORY FROM THE FIELD

Debra Gladstone is principal at Mineral Springs Elementary School in Winston-Salem, North Carolina. Ms. Gladstone did not ever think about being a principal, as her career as a probation/parole officer in Wake County and owner of two video stores kept her busy. Times changed, and she began teaching fourth grade and loved it. As principal, she is responsible for 100 staff members and 567 students. The school is a Title I school; 97% of its students receive free or reduced-price lunch; 48% are Hispanic, 41% are African American, 6% are White, and 5% are classified as "other." English language learners are abundant in all classrooms, so teachers are fluent in multiple languages. One of Ms. Gladstone's guiding principles is to never forget what the classroom is like and what the challenges are that face all teachers today. Being a principal is

> really a scary, scary thing. Oh my gosh! You have to wear so many hats and the work is never, ever done. The role of the principal is clear to me. I cannot just say "here you go" and expect my new teachers to survive. I have the responsibility to be relentless in helping nurture and support everyone so that my students are successful.

THE ADMINISTRATOR'S ROLE

When Ms. Gladstone took over at Mineral Springs Elementary School, she needed a plan for supporting her new and existing staff members. One of the first things she did was to make sure that everyone knew why they were there and that the children were their priority. They implemented PBIS (Positive Behavior Intervention System); created common, uninterrupted planning time for all grade levels; assigned mentors to new teachers; and assigned grade-level buddies to teachers with some experience.

Mineral Springs Elementary teachers meet every week to share ideas about instruction and what works or doesn't with their students. The new teachers also meet once a month with Ms. Gladstone and other administrators to share successes and challenges. This is a time during which the administrative team can gather information to help the new teachers grow and improve their teaching.

Ms. Gladstone's goal is to provide continuous and systematic support for her staff.

An effective principal plays a key role in helping each new teacher. This may include finding an appropriate mentor, providing professional development based on skills and knowledge needed, helping with classroom management, and managing the general logistics of teaching and planning. Arranging for time to collaborate with other teachers is also important, as these meetings and conversations lead to learning for all participants. In schools where principals actually work alongside their new teachers, morale is at a higher level than it is in schools where this is not the case.

Reynolds's (1995) review of research on learning to teach identifies four common limitations of beginning teachers. Leaders should be able to address these issues and provide strategies that can support effective teaching. These teachers often

1. have difficulty seeing the pedagogical implications of student differences and tailoring materials and instruction accordingly. They must learn about differentiation and understand that a one-size-fits-all approach to teaching is not effective.

2. are not able to "read" a class environment and establish appropriate rules and routines.

3. do not know a subject in ways that allow them to provide explanations to their students.

4. analyze their own teaching in ways that appear to be less focused than experienced teachers' reflections.

A study by Davis and Bloom (1998) showed that one aspect of principal support should be to guide new teachers in professional growth activities. Districts and schools provide multiple opportunities for teacher learning experiences, but seldom do these experiences focus on the skills and knowledge new teachers need. Quality professional development should be aligned with the day-to-day practices centering on instruction and assessment, management and organization, and collaboration and communication.

Misconceptions From New Teachers

If you are a sports fan, you will marvel at how easy it looks to kick a perfect field goal 50 yards, shoot and hit a three-pointer, or run a marathon and beat your record. Do you think you could do this and be successful without a lot of rehearsal and drill? What new teachers do on a daily basis is on-the-job training, and they do it without the benefit of years of practice.

As the leader of your district or school, you have the opportunity to make a difference in developing quality educators who stand in front of your students on a daily basis. We should consider the fact that new teachers don't know what they don't know and will enter your building with many preconceived notions about teaching. Learning how new teachers think about teaching is valuable in supporting the work in your building. Opinions about teaching vary from person to person, and having an open conversation about roles and responsibilities could be a starting point. I recently interviewed a group of administrators and mentors and asked them about their concerns in working with beginning staff members. They were very clear that new teachers have multiple misconceptions about teaching and that their awareness of these should help guide their work in designing new teacher support models.

Misconception 1: New teachers come ready to teach.

New teachers bring a sense of enthusiasm, high expectations, and fresh ideas to a school. They are energetic and optimistic when they enter the teaching profession. Many of them will teach the same way that they were taught, and this is often a reflection of their college courses. The classrooms today are very diverse. More children are in poverty, English is not their primary language, abuse persists, and violence is common. New teachers often come from a different background and are not prepared to face the realities of day-to-day classroom teaching.

Misconception 2: All children want to learn.

Catherine once told me that she could not understand why her students did not have the same passion for learning to speak French that she had.

Her disillusionment with teaching came quickly, as she was focused more on her own love of the language than on the need to manage and organize her classroom. Knowing how children learn and how to make connections with them is a critical piece in helping new teachers impact learning.

Misconception 3: Teaching is easy, and anyone can teach.

It used to be said that anyone who could not find a "real job" could teach. This is not the case anymore with the diversity in our schools. Many people are coming into education after their second or third career, and the differences between working with adults in a real-world business scenario and with students in a classroom are vast. Some people say that teaching is one of the hardest jobs ever, but all jobs are difficult at times. The problem is that teachers are dealing with students who often don't want to be in school. It is not just about making it fun but finding the one or two things that work for each student.

Misconception 4: The teaching day ends at 3:30.

Mr. Johnson was overwhelmed his first year of teaching. He was working more than 60 hours during the week just to plan and organize his day-to-day tasks. His family did not understand that this was normal for many new teachers and began to question why he had left a high-paying job to teach eighth-grade science. The list of things that he had to do was endless: lesson plans, team meetings, bus and hall duty, grading papers, returning parent calls and e-mails, writing the department newsletter—the list went on and on. He began to lose track of why he wanted to teach.

Misconception 5: Teachers get summer off, but administrators work all year.

In summer, teachers do not usually work the regular teaching hours, but the work does not stop for educators. Many new teachers are busy with additional jobs, doing coursework and attending professional development, developing new lessons, learning new technology, and often planning a family vacation. It is a time for more flexibility and self-selection of activities. As a leader, it is important to help guide your new staff members in selecting the best summer learning opportunities based on your observations and feedback during the year. You may also want to allow time for them to get into their classroom prior to the beginning of school just to get organized.

Misconception 6: The job of training new teachers is left to the assistant principal or someone else.

The role of the building principal has drastically changed over the years from that of a manager of books and buses to that of an instructional leader who is well versed in research-based information on best practices in teaching and learning. Today's leaders must take ownership of what priorities need to be addressed within their school and how to get things done with the resources given. One of my new teachers was very clear when she said, "The principal should be accessible and approachable." A study by the Wallace Foundation (Louis, Leithwood, Wahlstrom, & Anderson, 2010) found that, "When principals and teachers share leadership, teachers' working relationships with one another are stronger and student achievement is higher."

Misconception 7: New teachers are prepared for anything.

In the world today, being safe at school has become a major focus for all school community members. It is no longer the place where everyone can feel sheltered and protected from the outside world. Several new teachers have said that their principals were outstanding in providing "what to do if" scenarios during their orientation. It is important to remember that your new staff may not be from your area and aware of the natural hazards that may occur during the school year. These include fire, tornado, and earthquake drills. In addition, teachers have talked about the need to know the verbal codes for lockdowns or crisis drills and specifically what to do. One of my first-year second-grade teachers told the story of experiencing an earthquake for the first time and having to look at 28 children and reassure them that they would be safe when she was not so sure herself. Another teacher was terrified of dogs, and seeing the drug dogs checking high school lockers made her quit on the spot.

Misconception 8: Technology is your friend.

The days of blackboards and chalk are almost gone. Technology and all the gadgets to go with it have arrived. Teachers are encouraged and expected to use the new tools in engaging and productive ways in the classroom. Many new teachers are well versed and feel comfortable in using the Internet, slideshow software, wikis, and Facebook along with the computers and tablets provided by school districts. But things break and crash, so it is important to have a backup plan. If the bulb in the projector burns out (and it will), there has to be another way to keep the momentum going in the classroom. And if there are budget issues, there may be no funds for getting additional bulbs.

Misconception 9: There are better jobs out there.

While this may be true, there may not be more rewarding ones. From the courageous teachers in schools of crisis to those in schools where natural disasters occur, educators always go above and beyond their job description to help children. Educators do an endless list of things that support and nurture our young people. For those who stay with it over time, the rewards are fulfilling despite all the battles and challenges. You may never know the impact you make on a student until years later, but you will be inspired to continue to make a difference every day.

A New Teacher Support Model

Do you recruit or retain? Is it better to have a site-based new teacher support process in place before you actually need it? Does your process address the developmental needs of each individual? If the program doesn't have a strong, unwavering commitment from you, your new teachers might not make it.

I began my career in education as a junior high science teacher. After 18 years in the classroom, I became a program specialist for gifted and talented students, and finally I became a regional assistant superintendent for K–12 schools. My task was to improve teaching and learning in a diverse set of schools. My job description did not include new teacher support, but with 92% first-year teachers in these schools, I saw an opportunity to make a difference in how we developed quality educators. My boss, at the time, allowed me to design and implement a new teacher support model but not on the district's time. So each morning, starting at 7:00 a.m., I was conducting professional development for my new teachers targeted at the skills and knowledge they needed.

My goal was to have our new teachers want to return each day and ultimately for years. A seamless flow of professional development targeted at specific skills established a yearlong goal of retention.

As you consider your role in new teacher support, reflect on the following ideas:

- Do you provide teachers with an open door policy and access to you with time to share and discuss issues, concerns, and successes without fear of retaliation or embarrassment?

- What kind of sustained professional development do you provide that is relevant, standards based, and grade-level specific?

- How do you support teachers with research-based strategies, including in the areas of organization, classroom management, instruction, and assessment?

- How do you improve the level of teacher satisfaction regarding working conditions and school climate?

- What kind of culture, with high expectations and celebrations, do you establish?

- How do you improve student achievement by improving the quality of teaching?

- How do you build the capacity for teachers to serve as mentors for new teachers?

Helping our new teachers prepare for their first year will make their teaching career much more effective and productive. If you think back to when you began your teaching and all the things you wished you had known, you will generate a long list of items. During my new teacher support seminars, I have worked with more than 500 new teachers in 19 K–12 schools. The elementary group had college certification, which meant that they had taken courses in methodology and content and had completed some kind of student teaching at a chosen grade level. My middle and high school group, on the other hand, was composed of first-year teachers who were hired via "lateral entry," which meant they had a degree but no educational coursework or experience. We actually hired teachers off the street and assigned them to a school and grade level based on a vague alignment to their degree. The truth was that they really had no clue what to do or how to do it.

When looking at what new teachers need, the answer is everything. The number-one topic is classroom management. Other areas of need include the following:

- Opening and ending the school year

- Classroom environment

- Relationship building with staff, students, and the community

- Standards aligned to units of study and lesson plans

- Instructional and assessment strategies

- Stress management

- Conflict resolution

- Testing and a code of ethics

- Observation and evaluation

Our monthly seminars were designed to build the skills and knowledge new teachers needed for a successful first year. We held the sessions at various school sites, and everyone had the goal of becoming an exemplary teacher. Our first session was a day-long workshop before school started, in which several principals and I provided strategies and activities that would help with planning for the first week. Principals were required to attend and learn additional strategies to help with classroom implementation. We spent time helping the teachers get to know their school building, learn the logistics of getting supplies and materials, figure out how to set up their classroom, and a multitude of other things. One of the favorite activities was a school scavenger hunt. New staff were teamed up and given a sheet that listed people, places, and things to find in the school. We had great prizes for the winning team (and everybody else). They learned where the nearest restroom was, the names of the main secretary and custodian, what emergency procedures were, and where supplies were located. It was one of the strategies that allowed our new staff to feel more comfortable with the building and the people working in the school. About two months into the school year, one of my new fourth-grade teachers called me around 11:00 in the evening. I really didn't understand why, until she explained that she had experienced her first student with projectile vomit, and she knew who to call for help and how to get help. I told her how proud I was of her and thanked her for being so ready in a case of emergency.

A good amount of research has gone into adult learning and the best practices for providing professional development to adults. Those of us who do professional development on a regular basis know that teaching adults can be much more difficult than teaching students. The professional development that you plan in your district or school should consider the following:

1. **Adults have prior knowledge related to education.** This includes K–12 experiences and post–high school coursework. New teachers will often emulate their previous teachers, and depending on the quality of these educators, this experience can either make or break a classroom teacher. Two scenarios are observed here: Either they will lecture or they will be more hands-on and engaging.

2. **Adults want to know *why* they are learning something and have a what's-in-it-for-me attitude.** There has to be a reason for attending any professional development, and there must be a connection made back to the classroom in order for adults to make sense of what is being presented. This goes back to the what's-in-it-for-me question that is often posed by workshop participants.

3. **Adults have different learning styles and needs, including visual, auditory, and kinesthetic modalities.** Visual learners like graphs, charts, diagrams, video clips, and illustrations. New teachers who are visual learners will often be in the front of your meetings. Auditory learners listen and will make decisions based on your voice tone and level. They will enjoy a question and answer session. Kinesthetic learners need to move and will not sit still. Role-playing and incorporating them as volunteers help with their learning.

4. **Adults want to be social.** We all know that teaching adults can be challenging and that teachers, more than any other group, like to talk. Having time to share thoughts and self-reflect during professional development sessions will allow for opportunities to be involved with their learning.

5. **Adults want to know what is expected of them in relation to their job and how they will be held accountable for their work outcomes.** Agendas and invitations to workshop sessions will provide the learning experiences and outcomes for your professional development. You must be very clear regarding what you expect once the sessions are over and what type of accountability you will have for the implementation of the skill or knowledge acquired at the session.

6. **Adults want feedback.** This must be timely, specific, relevant, and constructive. Like students, adults need to know what they are doing well

and what areas they need to grow in. Leaders must take time to observe and provide small, incremental doses of feedback for change to occur. Too much can overwhelm a new teacher who is trying to learn how to do everything from management to organization to instruction to assessment.

Potential Roadblocks

Implementing a new teacher process is an exciting and productive journey and leaders must take ownership to create an effective system for support. Leaders around the country have shared several roadblocks that can hinder the implementation of a support model. Figure 2.1 provides several factors to consider. Take time to reflect on each and on whether it presents obstacles to you.

Figure 2.1 **Potential Roadblocks**

Factors to Consider	Reflection
Implementation of a new teacher support model	
Teacher evaluation systems	
Resources	
Time to meet (group and individual)	
Differentiation by levels of expertise	

(Continued)

Figure 2.1 **(Continued)**

Factors to Consider	Reflection
Content knowledge	
Technology skills	
Mentors and coaches	
Instructional planning teams	
Administrator/staff conflict	
Funding	
Paperwork, forms, and compliance requirements	
Standards, curriculum, and lesson planning	

Figure 2.1 **(Continued)**

WHAT ELSE CAN I DO?

Before beginning or supplementing a new teacher support process, take time to remember who is in your building and how their backgrounds and experiences can make or break their success with teaching. Many of these new educators will view teaching as a short-term career and be unsatisfied with the multiple aspects of the job. With a generation of teachers now retiring, the need to be more aware of how to help educators make teaching a lifelong career is critical. One new high school teacher interviewed recently stated,

> If I don't like where I am, I will leave. No question about it. Life is too short to not enjoy coming to work every day.

Schools are very diverse in their teaching populations, with new teachers being defined in so many ways, including by race, gender, and ethnicity. Some of your new staff will be straight out of college, some will be coming into a second or third career, some will have no educational background in teaching, and some will be experienced teachers who are changing locations. More than one third of today's educators have worked in another profession before moving into teaching. This is a time in which we have four or more generations working together for the first time in history. Each group has values and attributes that it brings into the school community. As you look at your new staff members, identify the differences in how they approach teaching and learning in four areas: work, personal life, loyalty, and authority. It is important to understand the impact that these can have on relationships, communication, and student learning.

According to Howe and Strauss (2003) in *Millennials Go to College*, there are groups of people who can be defined by their birth years and characteristics. A generation is defined as a 20- to 22-year span which includes significant events, characteristics, strengths, and challenges. Each group is defined by its experiences, and it is important to understand how each plays a role in building a culture of collaboration and communication within your building. Howe and Strauss's generations include the following:

- The Lost Generation (1883–1900)
- The G.I. Generation (1901–1924)
- The Silent Generation (1925–1942)
- The Boom Generation (1943–1960)
- Generation X (1961–1981)
- The Millennial Generation (1982–2001)

Figure 2.2 shows the categories, strengths, and challenges related to each group. Strategies are provided to give you suggestions for supporting each group of teachers.

Figure 2.2 Strategies for Generations

Category	Strengths	Challenges	Strategies
Silent Generation (Veterans and Traditionalists)	Loyal, respect for authority, consistency, practical, trusting, logical, prefer paper/pencil communication, dedicated, patient, rule followers, will work within the system but not change it	Need structure and organization, are challenged by technology, dislike change, have experienced the most change in life, will often lecture, take time to learn new skills	• Provide agendas, bulleted or outline form with concise points • Review important points • Provide clear expectations, support technology integration and learning • Value their experiences and their perseverance
Boom Generation	Loyal, workaholic, goal oriented, people pleasers, social, dedicated, problem solvers, health oriented, dislike authority	Must be appreciated and recognized, have elder relatives, "big picture" people, team players, like to explore, process learners, sensitive to feedback	• Provide time to practice every new skill • Provide teaming/mentoring time, organize materials in outline format with concise information embedded • Recognize their contributions • Tell them you need them often • Provide lots of interaction for collaboration • Encourage competition
Generation X	Nontraditional, technology oriented, self-reliant, "work to live" attitude, risk takers, like change, global thinkers, informal, learn by doing, like visual communication such as graphics and PowerPoints	Child care issues, distrusting, feel others owe them something, hard to motivate, want constant and specific feedback, dislike group and teaming time, cynical and impatient with interpersonal skills	• Pay attention to their personal lives • Provide extra support and attention • Provide graphics and visuals • Encourage opportunities for risk taking • Allow individual reflection time • Allow time to learn new skills • Provide opportunities for fun
Millennial Generation	Curious, lifelong learners, team players, problem solvers, communicators (by technology), confident, overachievers, materialistic, optimistic, accepting of others	Need support and supervision, very social, need friends, need peer opinion and feedback, multitaskers, no use for paper/pencil, not always obsessed with work	• Use lots of technology • Allow them to be creative and present information • Provide resources and relevant articles • Allow them to work with others • Tell them they are important • Provide opportunities to socialize • Recognize diversity in this group • Allow them to try new things on their own

   While it is impossible to create individual plans to address every need, valuing these differences will allow you to build relationships and understand how to manage your working time with the staff. Ask for input from all groups, and allow each to make contributions on a regular basis.

   Ynez Olshausen, of Waddell Language Academy, realizes that with the diversity of her international team of teachers, she must approach staff development in a variety of ways in order to address the multiple learning needs of her multinational staff. While she recognizes the different generations, her mission is to make the school a 21st century learning environment and create a global society with the skills and knowledge needed to function in any situation. Her communication with staff, students, and parents involves multiple modes that help her diverse population understand the vision and mission of the school.

SELF-REFLECTION QUESTIONS

Take time to reflect on the questions in Figure 2.3 related to your role as a leader and your support of your new teachers. Your responses in both the strengths and challenges columns should help guide you with implementing strategies that will impact your school community. You should be able to chart your journey as the instructional leader as you progress through the year.

Figure 2.3 **Self-Reflection Questions**

Reflection Questions	My Strengths	My Challenges	My Strategies
How do I create a welcoming and collegial work environment that values the characteristics of my new staff members?			
How have I involved experienced teachers to support our new staff?			
How have I provided every new teacher with a daily individual planning time during the school day?			

(Continued)

Figure 2.3 (Continued)

Reflection Questions	My Strengths	My Challenges	My Strategies
How have I provided time for my new staff to collaborate with other highly effective teachers and with their mentors?			
How have I provided duty-free time for my new teachers?			
How do I support my new staff during grade-level planning time?			
How have I contributed to grade-level meetings with agendas, objectives, and time for meeting?			
How have I structured the teaching schedule so that my new teachers have realistic assignments?			
How do I value progress over process?			

Building Relationships

QUOTE

I'm listening.

—Mr. Calvin Wallace,
regional superintendent

STORY FROM THE FIELD

Mr. Calvin Wallace is an exemplary leader. In his long educational career, he has been a teacher, administrator, regional superintendent, and interim superintendent of the Charlotte-Mecklenburg school system. He was a key writer for the North Carolina ABCs accountability model, which was the beginning of the standards movement that would guide curriculum development in the 1990s. He became a regional superintendent, and I had the opportunity to work with him for five years in what was known as Region B in the Charlotte-Mecklenburg school system. We were in charge of 24 schools, and 21 of them were low performing by all local, state, and national standards. There were 19 first-year principals, and 92% of the K–12 teaching staff were first-year teachers. We had a sense of urgency to improve leadership with the administrators and teaching with the classroom educators and to do this quickly as instructed by the superintendent.

Every day, Mr. Wallace would walk the halls of one of his schools. He spent about half of his time at the central office and would visit each school on a regular basis to talk with the administration and staff. When he entered a building, he was noticed. Not for his stature or title but for his presence. There was not a person that he didn't speak to, call by name, and inquire about their personal life and family. He would always visit the cafeteria workers and the custodial staff and speak about their work. We would often go to kindergarten classes and read with the children. He always laughed but loved the fact that I would carry a four-foot stuffed moose with me to share during story time. Of all the people with whom I have worked, he is one of the most respected, valued, and professional person.

THE ADMINISTRATOR'S ROLE

I can tell the culture of a school building within about 30 seconds of walking in the front door. In schools with effective cultures, there is an atmosphere that students come first, and adults model the respect and core values that are important for effective schools. The front office staff is welcoming and friendly, and safety is a priority. The principal is probably not in the office, teachers are monitoring halls during class changes, and students clearly understand the expectations for learning and behavior. Theodore Roosevelt's old saying, "People don't care how much you know until they know how much you care," is important to consider here. Building positive relationships within the school community is critical to a beginning teacher. Your teachers must know that you are a part of their team, and knowing about each one as a person is the first step.

Those of you who are coaches know the stress that is placed on you and on the creation of a winning team. Many people have opinions about coaches and describe them as "great," "horrible," or "just need to be fired." They are told that they don't connect with their players, that their expectations are too low or too high, and that they have no interpersonal skills with which to deal with the general public. Some are too domineering while others are too passive in their relationships with their team members. They are just not with it, and the team is on a course of failure and loss. There are numerous stories of major league coaches who had to learn to connect with their players. Learning about their players as individuals, listening to their concerns, taking them out for fun, and focusing on what really mattered to them improved winning during the season. We live in a technology-dominated, fast-paced, impersonal society, and we need to remember that it is our *people* and our relationships with them that matter.

Ynez Olshausen at Waddell Language Academy builds relationships with her school community from the first day of school. Her teachers are from the United States, China, France, Germany, and Japan, and they come together to teach children foreign languages. The first day of school is fabulous, as students participate in an Olympic-style opening ceremony with parades, banners, and music. It is a positive start to a journey of learning. Olshausen often says that she models her philosophy after the work of Rudolph Giuliani in looking at leadership styles and the way they represent their stakeholders. His implementation of a zero-tolerance policy has inspired her to develop a similar concept at Waddell. In a school with 1,400 students, she and her staff are consistent with the message that they like to "harass children for the low-level stuff," such as hats, saggy pants, visible cleavage, and running in the halls. The idea is to stop something before it escalates into something bigger. If the staff can positively reinforce what people value and respect as a society, then they can create high expectations for a climate that is safe and orderly.

Many districts have surveys that teachers, parents, and students complete each year to provide administrators with data regarding how well a school is operating. Each principal has the opportunity to use this information to make changes or continue with the processes within the building. Olshausen has a unique way of looking at challenge by looking at the quality of the complaints. Her faculty advisory committee meets with her to share the issues in the building that need attention. The way that she addresses these issues determines how effective she is as a principal and how effective the relationships are that she builds in the school. You often hear her saying, "I value how we do things," "thank you," and "I share your concerns." This reinforces the fact that she is listening to her teachers and that she is aware that there is a problem. Her response to complaints is based on what is and what is not within her control. One teacher complained about the color of the walls in the workroom, and although the color was horrible, it was not within her control. Another teacher complained about the inconsistency and safety of afterschool dismissal. This could be resolved within the building. However, both issues deserved a response, and how it was handled determined whether the conversations were positive or not.

Every Friday morning is special at Waddell Language Academy. Olshausen reads a story aloud to the entire school via closed-circuit television, sharing great literature from around the world. With the international staff and children who may have never left the county, she is valuing the diversity and providing learning opportunities for everyone. She models the guided reading process with guiding questions that teachers will discuss with the students after the television broadcast, which includes relevant vocabulary. Through the use of maps and globes and related vocabulary, she shows students where the story is from and expands their world through the wonder of travel. Her "think about" and "what if" questions stimulate curiosity and the love of reading and sharing.

New Teachers and Relationships

It is a scary moment when a new teacher stands in front of students for the first time. So many of them say that they want their children to like and respect them, follow the rules, and learn something during the year. Building a positive rapport in a classroom is the first step to successful teaching. So many teachers tell me that they reflect about the day on the way home. They think about how they did, what worked and what didn't, and ask themselves if they would want to be a student in their classroom. Students have an uncanny ability to size up a teacher in just a few minutes. They quickly take inventory of the room and decide if the atmosphere is welcoming or cold. They look at all of the visuals, including the posters, lights, living and nonliving animals, plants, and other items that catch their attention. One of my middle school math teachers openly admitted that his classroom atmosphere skills were dismal. He asked for help in decorating so that the room would be a place where math was valued and learned. One of the first things we did was cut out construction paper numbers and put them around the walls. We added math quotes and pictures of places where math was used in the real world. He asked students to bring in things for the bulletin board and added student work on a regular basis. Not only did this confirm his love for math, it gave students a role in building their classroom learning community.

Building relationships with students includes everything that surrounds the student, including sounds, smells, visuals, and teacher presence. The classroom should be student centered. The teacher desk should not be the cornerstone of the room but used as a tool. The arrangement of the desks should be conducive to movement, and learning areas should be clearly marked and supported with rules and procedures. Reading nooks are common in so many classrooms and provide a safe haven for children to go to relax and enjoy a good book or story. Student work should be displayed in the room and halls so that students know effort is valued.

I met a brand-new math teacher in one of the most challenging middle schools in the country. He had a degree in math but no educational experience or coursework in teaching. The human resources department looked at his degree and just plopped him into this school. He grew up in the projects of a large inner city, where children had little or no chance of getting out. His family's commitment to his education was strong, and he was one of the first to go to college and graduate. He wanted to give back and left another job to teach. On the first day of school, I walked into his room and heard him say, "This is a 92% class. Ninety-two percent of you will come to school every day; 92% of you will do your homework, be on time, and respect each other and me." I was curious about the choice of 92, and he told me that he knew that his students would make a mistake and was allowing for that in a dignifying way. It was ironic that at the end of the year when I heard him tell them that 92% would pass the end-of-course algebra test, all of his students corrected him, saying that it would not be a 92% but a 100% pass rate. They were right.

As you are thinking about new teachers and how to help them build relationships, consider the following:

- New teachers need a sense of humor, but they should not be sarcastic.
- New teachers need support and guidance and a sense that they are not alone in this profession.
- New teachers will encounter success and challenges on an hourly/daily basis.

- It takes time to become an effective educator.

- New teachers don't understand the impact that building relationships and effective management can have on their teaching success.

- New teachers lose the fantasy of teaching during the first week and wonder how they will make it through the year.

- New teachers often don't want to ask for help or admit failure.

- Nothing really prepares a person for the first day of teaching.

Mr. Jay Posick is the principal at Merton Intermediate School in Merton, Wisconsin. His school has around 430 students in grades 5–8 and is led only by himself and his teachers. His enthusiasm and commitment to quality are very clear in his voice and actions within the building. After he has met with his Response to Intervention team, which is dealing with a student and his research project on a Chromebook, he can be found on the playground, dressed warmly, as it is the middle of winter. His relationships with his staff are strong, and there is a culture of respect, risk taking, and support that permeates his school. He has an open door policy, and there is a calendar on his door where teachers can sign up for individual chats. His philosophy of "I can't run my school behind my desk" is clear as he walks the halls and teaches classes when needed, and all is conducted using the "Merton Way." He attends weekly team meetings during a common planning time and encourages everyone to share how they can continue to support the academic and social growth of the students. And he tries to remember to turn off his technological devices when meeting with anyone.

One of his strategies is to give his teachers uninterrupted planning time each month so that they can discuss teaching and learning based on the needs of their students. During the time they are planning, the 430 students gather in the gym to hear motivational and engaging stories that align with the vision and mission of the school. He challenges himself with a "word of the year" and shares his experiences as he targets the impact that this word has on his school community. This year the word was *focus*. Several of his teachers decided to also take the challenge of finding a term that would guide their professional lives, and they chose words such as *integrity, appreciation, heart,* and *try*. Being able to interact with his staff and students on a daily basis fuels his desire to become a better and better principal.

All of us have an obligation to help new staff members develop positive relationships with students, colleagues, and parents and the school community.

1. Students

One of my favorite strategies is called Morning Meeting. It is based on the book, *The Morning Meeting Book: Strategies for Teachers*, by Roxann Kriete (2014). Although I started teaching before this book was published, I found that it just made sense to greet and welcome my students each day.

We always began class with a quick sharing of successes, accomplishments, and celebrations from the previous day. It set the tone for respect, listening, and valuing each student as an individual. I will never forget the morning that I forgot to recognize Emily's new hair color. She changed it so often, but failing to notice a new change was not a good move on my part. An introductory activity to the lesson allowed students a chance to warm up and get ready for learning.

As we look at the diverse nature of our schools, we must consider who our students are and what their backgrounds are. The book *The Skin That We Speak: Thoughts on Language and Culture in the Classroom* by Lisa Delpit and Joanne Kilgour Dowdy (2002) brings to attention an awareness of the language and literacy differences in children. Both teachers and students respond to people who are different from themselves. Barriers or misunderstandings often develop when we don't understand how our speaking voice and nonverbal actions impact our relationships with others. One of my first-year teachers was from Germany and had a thick accent. He was placed in a very challenging inner city school and had multiple problems with communication and management in his sixth-grade language arts classroom. He entered the school with no prior knowledge of the student population or of adequate teaching methodologies that would impact student learning.

I suggest that you talk with your new teachers about how to establish a good relationship from the first day. They may have the content knowledge but may not know how to build a rapport with people they have never met. Many new teachers think that teaching is a popularity contest or that they should be friends with the students. Popular and well-liked teachers are consistent and fair, and they listen to their students. If teachers want respect from their students, they must model what respect looks and feels like in the classroom. It is about approval, admiration, and confirmation of who we are and what we want to be, and it addresses the socioemotional needs of our students. Here are several ideas that you, as the administrator, should model with both students and staff, and share as strategies with your new teachers:

- Welcome them into the building or classroom.

- Ask them about their weekend, sports event, or family gathering.

- Pronounce their names correctly.

- Say thank you, a lot.

- Smile.

- Notice something different.

- Apologize, and be sincere about it.

- Tell personal stories as analogies.

- Watch your language, as a sense of humor is appropriate, but sarcasm is not.

- Do not have favorites.

- Provide specific feedback about behaviors.
- Do not judge or criticize in front of others.
- Start every conversation with something positive.
- Alleviate fear and blame.

2. Colleagues

Teaching is no longer an isolated job in which you can just close your door and hope no one comes to see you. Since 1975 and the implementation of individualized education programs (IEPs), general and special education teachers are required to work together. You must be willing to do this, whether or not you like your colleagues, in order to improve student achievement. I once worked with a fourth-grade team, the members of which clearly had no use for each other. After about two months, I finally had a chance to share my observations and told them, "You are not here to be liked. You are here to teach these children. Whether you like each other or not is not my problem. My goal is to improve student achievement, and that is what we will do."

New teachers may be afraid to speak up during team meetings and may be scared to share ideas. What you do to create a teaming environment is important in helping your new staff become valued and respected members of your school community. Effective schools have a culture where teachers want to contribute in order to make a difference and take responsibility for all students. Administrators must have the skills and knowledge to direct a data-driven professional learning team with high-quality instruction and assessment at the core. Think about the following strategies:

- Articulate your vision and mission often.
- Define what collaboration is, and model it.
- Collect a lot of data, and analyze them for strengths and challenges.
- Provide uninterrupted time for planning and collaboration, and use it productively.
- Listen to conversations, and watch for body language.
- Remember it is all about the students.
- Establish norms for all meetings, and review them at each session.
- Determine roles and responsibilities for each team member, and hold team members accountable.
- Use the rules of brainstorming for your meetings.

3. Parents and the School Community

New teachers often have a difficult time communicating with parents about their students. Cultural differences, language barriers, and lack of time are barriers that beginning educators face as they try to make the school–home connection work for them. Effective communication within the school community is essential for building a strong educational environment. How schools and teachers communicate affects the quality of student learning. Teachers are the ambassadors for their school, and what they do determines the perception that others have of the staff and school environment. Too often, the only times parents hear about their students is when bad things have happened, and they feel discouraged about how to help their children. It is important that leaders help new teachers focus on the positive aspects of their students and share that with parents or guardians. One of my new teachers used e-mail and the phone to celebrate good things and positive behaviors in the classroom. Classroom expectations were described as observable student actions and written on individual cards, which were kept in a bowl in her room. These included being on time, having a pencil, having homework, and bringing their books. Student names were written on craft sticks, which were stored in a cup. Each morning, she would draw a card from the bowl and a stick from the cup. If the student named on the stick met the expectation written on the card, she sent an e-mail or made a phone call to let the parents know how pleased she was that the student was achieving.

We all know that parent involvement is defined in hundreds of ways. How you define parent involvement will determine how you help support your new teachers in communicating and collaborating with parents and guardians outside the classroom. New teachers should consider including the following in their communication:

- What are we learning in our class

- How the child is meeting the goals or the standards

- The child's strengths and areas in need of improvement

- How the parents can help at home with their child's learning

The world is full of parents who want to see their child succeed and do better than they did. They are looking for ways to help and often do not have the answers or know what to do. The more parents and teachers share information that is relevant, language-appropriate, and aligned with the child's needs, the better the relationship will be to help the child meet behavioral and academic goals.

Chris Pearson is the principal at West View Elementary School in the Burlington-Edison School District in Washington. It is a preK–6 dual language school, where the mission is "Cada Niño," or "Each Child." Pearson began his career as a teacher and also served as a dean of students prior to becoming the leader of West View in 2011. The school is a Title 1 school that serves predominately low-income Hispanic students, and more than 79% of the school's students qualify for free or reduced-price lunch. In 2010, the school was identified as low performing and placed on the "priority" federal list. After the staff made a commitment to improvement and did a lot of work, West View was honored by the Washington Education Association in 2013 as a "High-Performing Priority School" and featured in the *Seattle Times* for its reading proficiency scores. Mr. Pearson and his staff were able to improve the reading proficiency from 40.1% to 62.5% in two years. The school was one of only 34 in Washington to achieve double-digit growth in both math and reading scores. In 2014, Mr. Pearson was named Washington State Elementary Principal of the Year, and he attributes his success to the strong partnership between the school and its community.

Mr. Pearson has been a principal for eight years and is a visible leader in the building; he believes in face-to-face communication with his teachers and students and greets everyone by name. He tells everyone that he has found his niche in the elementary grades, and it is apparent that he enjoys his role in supporting and nurturing his young students. Safety is a priority, and because West View is a Positive Behavior Intervention School, the goal is make sure everyone feels safe by the principal having a proactive presence in the building. To help support his staff and their needs, Mr. Pearson has established protected time for teachers to meet every Friday, allowing for a collaborative model where the needs of the children come first. New and veteran teachers discuss best practices that are individualized by the needs of the child. The time is spent problem solving and providing feedback on what is working and what should be improved. Mr. Pearson clearly says that if staff have a challenge, then it is their responsibility to run with it and find a solution. This is their fourth year of instructional teaming, and he says, "This is our fourth year of learning."

His teachers vary from new (right out of college) to veteran. Mentors provide support in both professional and personal areas. Each new teacher has a mentor with whom she or he meets in formal and informal settings, such as during school or for coffee afterward. In order to help teachers make connections with the community, the school established the Family Center, where families can access technology and complete GED classes, and English language learner students get tutoring support from volunteers and teachers. The Family Center brings the school together to provide services that help with student and parent learning needs. Mr. Pearson sees his role as an advocate for both, and he knows that this connection will help his teachers continue to have strong relationships with students in the classroom.

And the school has a waiting list for enrollment.

As the administrator, you must decide on the best strategies for communication and not be afraid to try new ideas and methods to increase parent involvement. The complexity of school-to-home communication has changed over time, as new technology has influenced our decisions on how to contact parents and guardians. The most effective forms of communication include conferences, phone calls, and e-mails, but in order to reach all of your families with their busy schedules, he asks teachers to consider several of the following as strategies during the year:

- Contact with parents before school starts to talk about yourself, your classroom, and expectations for success

- Parent conferences with breakfast or snacks

- Student-led conferences

- Parent-teacher organizations or school community councils

- Positive phone calls

- E-mail or school website

- Curriculum nights or "how do I teach this at home" evenings

- Home visits (when appropriate)

- Newspaper articles and celebrations

- Doughnuts for Dad or Muffins for Mom

- Homework hotlines

- Sports or other events (plays, special programs, field trips)

WHAT ELSE CAN I DO?

Ask your teachers to reflect on whether they would want to be in their classroom and why or why not. It is important to remember that a teacher's presence, voice tone, and nonverbal communication can determine effectiveness in teaching. Help them understand that their classroom is an extension of who they are, and that the values and beliefs they model are transferred to their students.

- Talk with your new teachers before the first day of school to share your expectations for classroom climate and atmosphere.

- Discuss the impact that body language has on building relationships. Talk about their stance, hand movement, eye contact, and walk patterns within the room.

- Model the best practices for using music in the classroom.

- Observe and provide specific feedback on the arrangement of the room, displays, cleanliness, and student access to materials.

- Emphasize the importance of student self-reflection and how it should be done on a daily basis. Model an approach to "I have something to share" when you talk about your learning for the day, so that teachers can use this in their classroom.

- Talk about the physical characteristics of setting up their classroom.

- Teach positive reinforcement through the use of Five-Second Cheers. These could include a high-five, pat on the back, round of applause, silent cheer, or another fun recognition activity.

- Model and practice positive reinforcement strategies for celebrating success.

- Provide examples of classroom displays that highlight student work samples.

- Take staff on a "classroom reflection walk" (see Figure 3.1) to look at other teachers' classrooms and see what ideas they can take back to use in their own rooms. Have them write notes to the teacher as they visit each classroom.

SELF-REFLECTION QUESTIONS

Take time to reflect on the questions in Figure 3.2 related to your role as a leader and your support of your new teachers. Your responses in both the strengths and challenges columns should help guide you with implementing strategies that will impact your school community. You should be able to chart your journey as the instructional leader as you progress through the year.

Figure 3.1   **Classroom Reflection Walk**

Classroom Observation	Comments, Ideas, and Suggestions
Classroom appearance	
Classroom arrangement	
Displays, informational boards, student work	
Materials, resources, supplies	

Figure 3.2 Self-Reflection Questions

Reflection Questions	My Strengths	My Challenges	My Strategies
How do I introduce myself to my new staff?			
How do I get to know my staff better?			
How do I balance the professional and the personal connections?			
How do I remove barriers so that teachers have the chance to teach?			
How do I show I value my staff?			
How do I define effective decision making in my school?			
How do I share decision making?			

(Continued)

Figure 3.2 (Continued)

Reflection Questions	My Strengths	My Challenges	My Strategies
How do I see myself as a master teacher and role model for my staff?			
What do I look for in an inviting, welcoming classroom? How do I share this?			
What relationship building skills do I need to refine?			
What do I do when I see a classroom that is not working in relation to student achievement or behavior?			
What do I do when adults bully each other?			
How do my teachers perceive me as an instructional leader?			

New Teachers and Stress

STORY FROM THE FIELD

I have worked with schools in rural, suburban, and urban areas of the country. I had the chance to work with a principal of a very challenging middle school in an inner city, urban area. She had been assigned to the school to "fix it" after numerous administrators had failed to turn the school around. Her school was in crisis, and she needed multiple solutions to deal with the overwhelming problems that faced her school community. One of her issues was the overwhelming number of first-year, lateral-entry teachers. More than 95% of her staff were beginning educators with very little experience in teaching. They had college degrees but no formal training in classroom organization and management, and no instructional experience. When she called me, I immediately set up time to meet with her new teachers and talk about their concerns. The monthly seminars that we established ended up saving her new staff and helping her keep them. The seminar in February was held in the media center on a dark, cold, and rainy day. I had balloons, funnels, and nice clean kitty litter for the group to make their own "stress orbs." We also had foot massagers, bottles of bubbles, and a basket with toys for everyone to play with and have a bit of fun while munching on wonderful snacks and treats. One of my former students, who was a deputy sheriff, also joined us to talk about safety and precautions for those that liked to arrive early in the morning and stay late at night. This seminar was one of their favorites.

THE ADMINISTRATOR'S ROLE

How do you handle the stress of your job as a leader? Are you proactive or reactive? Do you have to-do lists that are a mile long in multiple places? Does your family understand your role? Education is a stressful job and one that is constantly in a state of change and often confusion. Recognizing that new teachers will face an incredible amount of stress during their first few years is one component of being an effective leader. There are things that you can control and things that you cannot control. Knowing the difference will make you understand how to help your new staff work through the highs and lows during their first year.

Perception Versus Reality

Have you thought about how the world of teaching is similar to and different from the business world? Many new teachers are shocked and in a state of disbelief when they learn that their perception of teaching is different from the real world of teaching. The problem comes from the fact that they are teaching children, and day-to-day, unexpected events always happen. Let them share what they think teaching will be like for them, and have a conversation about the similarities and differences.

You might include the following as similar to the real world:

- You must come to work on time or notify us if you are not coming.
- You must plan your work each day and anticipate a change of plans.
- You will experience success and failure.
- You will be liked by some and not liked by others.
- You must follow the rules.
- You cannot hit people, use inappropriate language, or use poor spelling or grammar.
- You must learn to communicate and collaborate with others.
- Your work will be observed and evaluated.

You might think about the differences:

- You will not have a lot of free time.

- You cannot go to the bathroom or eat when you want to.

- You will do things that are not in your job description.

- Your family and friends will not understand what you do or why you do it.

- You may not have a room, cubicle, or place to call your own.

- You will not get all of the materials and supplies you need.

- You will not get directions on what to do.

- The air conditioning and heat are often beyond your control.

- Technological items break and stay broken, sometimes for a long time.

Seven Things to Consider

Stress in teaching is an important issue, and if left ignored, it can trigger deeper and far more serious issues in terms of a person's health and general welfare. Think about a day, from start to finish, in your building. It would be interesting if you kept a daily flow chart of your high and low points during the day. What feelings did you have from the time you got up to the time you went to bed? Did you experience ups and downs during the day? What were the trigger points and how did you manage them?

1. New teachers want to be perfect.

We need to make sure our new teachers understand that they will make mistakes, and these mistakes are opportunities for learning and growth. Admitting a weakness is difficult for anyone, but the frustration that comes from not getting everything right is detrimental to teachers' effectiveness in the classroom. Ask what you can do to support them, and check with them to see if your support is working.

2. New teachers want to know everything at once.

Teaching children is a multitask process with many steps and learning curves. It is important to work with your new staff on one or two things at a time and not overwhelm them with too many things to learn. Based on your observations in the classroom, help them recognize what they can improve over time with practice. Then, move on to something else.

3. The to-do list gets longer and longer.

New teachers really try hard to please students and parents, create engaging lessons, manage the students, and have a healthy balance between work and home. I have seen a teacher's desk covered with various colored sticky notes with tasks to complete each day. As principal, you will need to help teachers set priorities that will make the difference with their teaching. Remember, the word *priority* means somebody or something that is ranked highly in terms of importance or urgency.

4. Teachers will push their limits.

No one wants to admit defeat, and teachers will sacrifice their personal well-being to be present in the classroom. First-year teachers typically are the least healthy in your building. They work late hours, neglect sleep and food, are exposed to germs that they have never encountered before, and don't know how to stop.

5. New teachers want to be in control.

There are some things that we can control and some that we cannot. Recognizing the difference and being proactive, rather than reactive, will help ensure that the day-to-day routines go smoothly. We must understand that schools are places that have unexpected events; teachers' responses to a crisis determine the level of chaos or calmness that results in everyone's safety.

6. New teachers do not know how to say no.

It is your responsibility not to give a new teacher additional roles and responsibilities. They want to be involved and cooperative with the school community, but overloading them with noninstructional jobs will cause a quick burnout.

7. New teachers don't know their stress points.

Being observant is paramount in helping new teachers deal with stress. Although you are not a doctor, there are signs to look for as your new teachers progress through the year. These include excessive fatigue, crying, changes in interpersonal relationships with students and colleagues, negative comments, and absenteeism.

An important piece of being an effective leader is recognizing when stress will most affect your new teachers. Use Figure 4.1 to help design your strategies for supporting them through these times.

In 1990, the California New Teacher Project published an article related to the phases that first-year teachers move through during the year (Moir, 2011). Your knowledge and recognition of these phases—from anticipation, survival, and disillusionment to rejuvenation—will help in the process of supporting your new staff and being able to provide strategies to help relieve some of the stress experienced at each phase. As you read the following scenario, think about what you see in your school during the span of a first-year teacher's year.

Figure 4.1   **Times of Stress and New Teacher Concerns**

Times of Stress	New Teacher Concerns
Before the school year starts	Uncertainty of what to do Meeting colleagues/mentors/administrators Understanding the paperwork Balancing family and work
Before the first day and week of school	Classroom management Organization of the classroom Unknown procedures/routines Being liked/respected/appreciated Understanding the content/curriculum standards How to teach/engage students Assessing (informal and formal) Lesson planning Diverse learners and meeting their needs
Observations and evaluations	What the principal expects The evaluation instrument Ratings: good or bad Feedback and what to do with it
Parent-teacher conferences	What to say, do, and have for the conference Language barriers Uncooperative parents/guardians
Crisis or significant event at school	What to do in an emergency How to get help/support
Testing	High expectations for student success Job security if students do not do well Testing code of ethics
Professional development and other requirements	Attendance Credit Accountability back in the school/classroom

Mr. Johnson was so excited to get a position as a middle-grades science teacher. After leaving a high-paying job, he wanted to make a difference in the lives of students. He had no formal education coursework and no experience working with students this age, and he had never done any student teaching. But he did have a desire to teach and anticipated a great year. This excitement lasted about two weeks, after which he realized that he did not have a clue what to do. Classroom management was the greatest challenge, but organization and instructional delivery were high on his list too.

At this point, Mr. Johnson began to struggle. His personal life conflicted with his professional life, and the day-to-day experiences were overwhelming. He was spending more than 60 hours a week on school-related tasks. Being at a school with a preponderance of new teachers was not an asset. There were few veterans, and none in science who could share lesson plans or resources with him. He was in "everything is a first" mode and survived minute by minute. The back-to-school night terrified him, and he knew that his parents would not appreciate a scared and incompetent first-year teacher. At one of our first seminars in August, I had actually had the first-year educators practice their "welcome back to school" speech and get feedback from their peers, but the memory of this practice did not seem to reassure him.

Around November, he began to question why he had left his wonderful high-paying career job. His disillusionment with the students and the administration, and the fact that things were not going very well, were constant threats to his mental and physical condition. With the winter months approaching, I was concerned about his health, as he was burning the candle at both ends. The time demands were very high, as he wanted to fully participate in the holiday presentations, sport events, and end-of-quarter parent-teacher conferences, as well as write updated parent newsletters. In addition, he was preparing for his first formal observation by his principal and felt very incompetent and totally unprepared for this evaluation. His principal was a first-year middle school principal who not optimally supportive because he too was learning to do his job. However, he was not giving up hope and learning new skills every day.

The fact that November and December included holidays helped Mr. Johnson make it through these months. He let me know that he would be going home for the holidays and that his mother would probably want to intervene in his new career choice. At the December seminar, we talked about the family influences that staff would experience during the holiday break. Career decisions are made during this time, and I fully expected to lose many of my new staff members.

Winter break came and went, and Mr. Johnson was back. After a time at home with his family and friends, he was refreshed and ready to start again. His time was split between doing fun personal things and reorganizing his classroom, materials, and strategies. His principal opened the building for teachers several days before students returned, so that teachers could, if they wanted, come in and prepare for the start of school in

January. Mr. Johnson's only comment was, "I did it. I made it through the first half!" One of the pieces that he worked on was the pacing of the curriculum, as he was very behind in teaching content prior to the state testing in May. He was also very worried about how he would be perceived if his students did not do well on the test. He began to explore new strategies to teach better.

Spring break in April was a turning point for Mr. Johnson, and after spending some time in a warm, vacation environment, he came back ready to finish the year. I asked him to sum up his year, and he stated,

> Being a first-year teacher is very difficult, because you have so many things going on at once. I tell people this is the hardest job I have ever had. You are stretched in so many directions. So that's it. I am basically trying to do whatever I can to get by. Having support is crucial from Lynn and my mentor, because they help you piece it all together. And without that you would lose your mind and burn out. Throughout this year I am learning how not to burn out. For me, I just want to do the best job I can, and I know I am not the best teacher at the moment. I am not trying to be. I am just trying to survive. I want to make it through the year and still have a job when I finish and be willing to come back next year which at this moment is a career move and I plan on staying with it for good.

At the end of the year, Mr. Johnson was committed to his career choice. He did return and became an exemplary teacher over time.

WHAT ELSE CAN I DO?

One of the activities we did every month at our new teacher seminars was a take time to reflect. We would share strengths and challenges and how much learning had been gained since our last meeting. Some of the new teachers kept a journal of thoughts, while others just wanted to talk and share. We would write what everyone said on chart paper and have discussions on how similar the experiences were within the grade levels. Classrooms can be a source of chaos or calm, and how teachers react to situations will determine what happens during a crisis. The types of emergencies vary, but being proactive, rather than reactive, is a critical management component.

Calvin Wallace always said that we should never make someone's job harder than it already is. One of our first tasks to help reduce new teachers' stress is to identify the factors that are the causes and determine if they are within the teacher's control. Is the stress short term or long term?

The Teacher Stress Survey (Figure 4.2) provides you with a set of stress-related statements that can serve as a starting point for discussions about how best to handle and manage stress. This is not an inclusive list but a

Figure 4.2 **Teacher Stress Survey**

Reflection Statement	Response
I feel stressed.	
I feel insufficiently prepared for this job.	
I get impatient with myself and others.	
I cannot handle more than one thing at a time.	
I just don't have enough time to do anything.	
I am not learning fast enough to keep up with the students.	
I take on too many things to do.	
I don't feel appreciated or valued.	
I have multiple to-do lists around my classroom and home.	
I struggle with classroom management.	
I don't think my students like or appreciate me.	
I worry about observations and evaluations.	

Reflection Statement	Response
I am beginning to not like my students.	
I have multiple students that I cannot reach.	
I lack control over my life.	
I need more support in _____ (area).	
I respond to stress in many ways, including _____.	
I don't want to come to school.	
I struggle with paperwork, lesson planning, and daily tasks.	
I have concerns working with my mentor and/or grade-level team.	
I think my family is suffering with my teaching load.	
I don't have any time just for me.	
I am not sleeping or eating well.	

place to begin confidential conversations. Consider the following suggestions to help you create an action plan for growth and improvement.

- Have your new teachers make a list of the things that are causing them stress. Divide the list into two sections: things they can control and things they cannot. Help them focus on the things that they can effectively deal with, and put aside the others.

- Take time to play and have a bit of fun. (For example, small toys and a bottle of bubble solution can provide a lot of entertainment.)

- Make a list of five things that have gone well each day. We tend to focus more on the negative than the positive. Have teachers share with a colleague who can energize the moment and provide support.

- Have new teachers discuss their stress points, and offer solutions for reducing in- and out-of-class tensions.

- Talk about the potential crisis issues that may occur during the year, including drills, emergency procedures, and dangerous occurrences that may happen within the school building. Although some events are beyond our control, make sure that your new teachers know exactly what to do.

SELF-REFLECTION QUESTIONS

Take time to reflect on the questions in Figure 4.3 related to your role as a leader and your support of your new teachers. Your responses in both the strengths and challenges columns should help guide you with implementing strategies that will impact your school community. You should be able to chart your journey as the instructional leader as you progress through the year.

Figure 4.3   Self-Reflection Questions

Reflection Questions	My Strengths	My Challenges	My Strategies
How am I helping my new teachers deal with stress?			
Am I the cause of their stress?			
Have I noticed that new teachers are absent often? What are the causes?			
Have I established a time to meet with each new teacher every month to talk about successes and challenges?			
How do we have a bit of fun each month?			

(Continued)

Figure 4.3 (Continued)

Reflection Questions	My Strengths	My Challenges	My Strategies
How do I know my support is working or not?			
How do I make sure they have the materials they need for the classroom?			
How do I create a personalized stress plan with strategies I know work for them?			
How do I remind them of why they chose teaching?			
Have I noticed a change in the behavior patterns of my new teachers?			

Before School Starts

QUOTE

I am coming from two other careers. Both involved dealing with machines, not young people. I am perfectly terrified to stand in front of a group of kindergarten students and act like I know something.

—Mr. Howard,
first-year kindergarten teacher

STORY FROM THE FIELD

New kindergarten teachers are just the best. They have a sense of compassion, and they are kind, caring, and patient beyond belief. In some cases, they are first-year teachers who love children but don't have a clue as to the nature of these little beasts. Mr. Howard began his educational career by student teaching in kindergarten. He was able to get a position at this grade level but was moved to second grade after three weeks of school due to enrollment numbers. His classroom was the stage of the multipurpose room, and each time the school had an assembly, he had to dismantle his room and move his students. After seven years and a lot of begging, he was able to move back to kindergarten. Although he was not new to teaching, he was new to children this age, and he was working with a new curriculum and different methodologies for teaching. He had forgotten how hard it was to actually communicate with five-year-old children and that directions had to be really, really simple. He told his students to line up at the door. Do you know how many doors there were in his classroom?

THE ADMINISTRATOR'S ROLE

Jennifer Moore is an assistant principal at William Blount High School in Maryville, Tennessee. The school has three buildings, six administrators, and 1,800 total students, 45% of whom receive free or reduced-price lunch. It is located in a rural area near Knoxville, and teacher turnover has varied during the years.

Moore is in charge of the new teachers and has taken on this role because she has watched new staff members "flounder out there" and has needed to intervene. Many of the teachers are coming from business careers such as a nurse practitioner, ROTC colonel, and welder. Each of these teachers knew content but had no teaching experience. Like many schools, William Blount High School conducts professional development for these new hires prior to other teachers arriving at the beginning of the school year; it also supports first-year teachers with meetings during the year, mentors, and other support systems. One of their key focus areas is the use of technology and helping the new teachers understand how to use the district website, grade book, attendance record system, and classroom materials.

As she reflected on her beginning teaching experience, Moore determined that she wanted to ensure that new staff members didn't have a bad first day. Her school decided to have students remain in homeroom for the entire first day of class. She has made it very clear that the first day at William Blount High School will set the precedent for the rest of the year. Since the students are usually on their best behavior on this day, teachers take advantage of the opportunity to talk to their students, discussing and modeling how the rest of the year will be. Expectations are clearly defined for everyone.

Rob Clark, the principal at William Blount High School, drives 50 minutes each day to come to school. He comes to work because of the people and the impact that the relationships make within the community. He also understands the need to keep teachers, as they can easily leave and go to a neighboring district that pays up to $5,000 more than his district. In an effort to retain them, he tries to build a culture of respect and commitment to success.

Paula Jones, the lead mentor at the school, talks about the need to have every student feel welcomed and valued. All students take a foreign language, and she teaches French. It is important for her to instill the love of learning and teaching in all of the adults in the building. She helps the new teachers understand that their class should be their students' favorite, but this is the philosophy for all classes. Students have a hard time deciding on which class really is their favorite, because they really love them all. It is a school where caring and collegiality are making a difference in student learning and achievement.

The First Day

Now is the time for the first day. You have spent a lot of effort getting everyone ready but know that you probably have missed something. Make a list of what your priorities are, and share these. You will want to work with the end of the first day in mind. What will have been accomplished by your new staff, and how did they do? How did you welcome them into the building on the first day? How will you plan to check on each of them during the day or after school? All of them will have a lot of questions after teaching only a few hours. Make sure that you have told them the expectations and how to get the answers to their new questions. It is important that you thank them for their first day and tell them that you look forward to seeing them back tomorrow.

You have a great opportunity to ensure that the opening of school happens smoothly and efficiently. Each year, Mr. Wallace (recall him from Chapter 4) and I would visit our 24 schools on the first several days, and every principal had to phone in to let us know how the first day went and what problems existed. It was always a good thing to hear how well planned and organized they were and that all of the hard work prior to the students coming had paid off in a successful start to a new year. There will be mistakes and things not done, but if you focus on what really matters for that first day and week, it will make your life much easier over time.

Use the checklist called Classroom Expectations (Figure 5.1) to provide a list of procedures that you want your new teachers to have in place for their classroom to function effectively. Remember to identify the most urgent need, make observations in the classroom, and provide feedback for support.

The First Week of School

Your new teachers are beginning an exciting career at your school. You must remember that everything that a new teacher does is a first, and how you prepare them to handle these situations will make the difference between success and failure. Think about all of the things that you needed to know your first day and how prepared you thought you were. It is good to remember that your new teachers come with a variety of experiences. Some are fresh out of college, with or without student teaching, and are ready to put into place all the theory and textbook learning from their professors. Others are coming to teaching after having careers in industry or business and with the mindset of the professional world. Many of them were not brought up in the same manner as their students and struggle to understand "where the kids are coming from."

Figure 5.1 **Classroom Expectations**

Desired Results	What Is Observed	What It Should Be	What to Do
Students are orderly when entering and exiting the classroom.			
Materials are ready for instruction.			
Front board shows essential information, including the date and the day's objective statement, essential instructional question, and homework assignment.			
Arrangement of furniture is conducive to movement.			
Lesson plans are visible and current.			

Desired Results	What Is Observed	What It Should Be	What to Do
Attendance records are completed accurately and quickly.			
Student attention is focused on the teacher in a quick and respectful manner.			
Student materials are ready and accessible for use.			
Students are held accountable for their behavior and work.			
Discipline plan is posted, including rules, rewards, and consequences.			

You may also find that some of your new teachers are actually hired after the school year begins and will need a crash course on the logistics of teaching in your building. All teachers bring a wealth of information for their first year. The problem is that most of it will fly out the door on the first day. Teaching is hard and unpredictable. One of my new teachers was very proud of the fact that he could tell me everything I wanted to know about Maslow's hierarchy of needs. Beginning with survival and moving through safety/security, love, ego/esteem, and finally reaching self-actualization, he told me that this was totally related to the world of teaching. While I agreed that the categories did somewhat align to the needs of a new teacher, his attitude was that he was a superior being for knowing the hierarchy. It only took one student to tell him that he looked like a "total geek" to burst that bubble. While we must provide a safe environment to nurture our new educators, we need to make sure to offer a healthy dose of real-world teaching examples. We want to tell the truth about what they know and don't know and then figure out what they need to survive and develop.

Planning and Preparation

Have any of you ever been to a wedding or had to plan for one? Ynez Olshausen uses this analogy to talk about preparing her school for the first day. The people have to be there and know what to do, the venue has to be ready, the materials and resources have to be on display, and Plan B must be known by all. She shares how difficult this actually is to establish and the necessity for a consistent set of procedures that govern the minute-by-minute actions of teachers and students. As with a wedding, you have to rehearse over and over, practice until you get it right, plan for everything, and know that you will forget something. It is stressful trying to get all of the pieces to work together. New teachers are often very anxious on the first day, so helping them be well versed in what to do and how to get help will eliminate some of their frustration.

Dr. Lynnice Carter is an assistant superintendent in the Pontotoc County School District located in northeast Mississippi and just west of Tupelo. The district is in a small, rural area that serves about 3,600 students in two K–12 campuses and a career and technology center. It comprises a large industrial area, including automotive and furniture businesses that are very supportive of the school community. The emphasis on teacher support begins before students arrive. New teachers are brought in the day before other teachers arrive for a fun and informative session that provides them with information needed to start the school year. Superintendent Kenneth Roye welcomes the new educators and sets the stage for the vision and mission of the district. Dr. Carter has planned a great day that includes the history of the district, information and tips for the first days, and a panel of teachers who share best practices. The best part of the day is called "If Only I Had Known," which is presented by a group of second-year teachers. They share the "real world of teaching" story about their survival during their first year. The day ends with an overview of the Mississippi Statewide Teacher Appraisal Rubric (M-STAR) and an introduction to the district website. Everyone leaves with a huge bag of goodies for their classroom and a feeling of excitement and readiness.

Sample Orientation Agenda From Pontotoc County School District

8:00–8:30	Welcome/District Challenge/Information
8:30–9:00	Who We Are
9:00–9:15	Break
9:15–10:15	Special Area Highlights
10:15–11:45	Teach 101/Best Practices
11:45–12:15	Catered Lunch
12:30–1:30	If Only I Had Known
1:30–1:45	Break
1:45–2:15	M-STAR (Mississippi Statewide Teacher Appraisal Rubric)
2:15–2:50	District Website
2:50–2:55	Evaluation
2:55–3:00	First-Day Jitters

WHAT ELSE CAN I DO?

The beginning of the school year is a wonderful time for everyone. There is an air of enthusiasm and renewal and a feeling that this will be a better year than the last one, that our hard work will lead us all to success in teaching that learning. You don't want to hear, "If only I had known that . . ." in your building. Setting the stage for success begins before the students actually come into the building. It is important to prepare your new staff with a toolbox of activities and strategies that will make the opening day a complete success. In working with new teachers over the years, I have seen principals take time to ensure that new staff are prepared in both organization and management of teaching.

Some years ago, I was working in a very large middle school with a less-than-desirable administrative staff. For some reason, the principal did not have any interest in her 37 new staff members. I had been conducting new teacher support seminars for several months and was visiting with these teachers to see how they were doing and what support I could provide. I was the classroom of one of my new teachers and knew that this teacher wanted to make it and survive his first year. I always loved being in his classroom, as he just had the passion for teaching. However, I noticed that his students were constantly leaving the classroom and returning. They were doing this very quietly, but the continuous flow was disruptive. I asked him why, and he told me that he had to let them go next door to sharpen their pencils. He had requested a pencil sharpener multiple times but had not received one. It took me less than three minutes to go and find one for him.

This section is about practical advice for supporting your new staff during the first days of school. These are real strategies that principals have used over the years with great success. You may already be doing some of these, but I hope that you can find several that you can try for next year. But most important, tell the truth. College courses talk about warm, friendly student-centered classrooms, but the reality of a first-year teacher's classroom may be very different. Model what you expect every chance you can, and make sure your new staff understand that what they learned in college or graduate school may not apply to their first year.

- Do not read the teacher handbook out loud to them. Point out salient passages, or design interactive tasks so that they learn the components that will help during the first week of school; the rest will come.

- Provide the procedures for filing forms, either paper or electronic.

- Take them on a school scavenger hunt in your building.

- Give them a "new teacher" box of goodies and supplies.

- Design an "I Really Need" request form that they can use to communicate needs with you.

- Provide a general list of supplies that they should have for their classroom.

- Model and provide several opening-of-school activities that they could use with their students during the first week (e.g., classroom scavenger hunt, people bingo).

- Have a classroom reflection walk. Once the classrooms have been decorated, arrange a walk so everyone can visit and see each other's classrooms.

- Arrange a time for first-year teachers to meet their mentor (if applicable). Review the protocols for meetings, getting support, observations, and confidentiality.

- Take time to review the curriculum standards. Make sure they have copies or electronic versions of what they will be teaching. If you are using units of study, review the format and design of these documents.

- Review your lesson planning procedure. If this includes a template, go over it, and explain your expectations and what they will be held accountable for. An example of an exemplary lesson plan could help guide their writing process.

- Go over the logistics of day-to-day teaching. This includes start and end times, getting substitutes, emergency protocols and phone numbers, and electronic filing of attendance records, grades, and other data.

- Review their noninstructional duties and responsibilities if you are asking them to do anything in addition to teaching. This could include supervision of students, attendance at meetings and extra-curricular events, parent contact, documentation, and class coverage for their colleagues.

- Go over the school rules, procedures, rewards, and consequences that support your behavior management plan. Make sure each new teacher knows how to get help when needed.

- Help them determine their classroom rules and procedures. Provide poster board for classroom display. If they are on a grade-level team, encourage consistency across the team on implementation. We expect them to know everything, but learning how to run a class-room takes a lot of time and perseverance. Some of your new staff may want to observe one of your master teachers and reflect on what they saw.

- Several suggestions for having teachers practice the student routines are listed:
  - Entering and exiting the classroom
  - Lining up to go in or out of the classroom
  - Moving through the halls
  - Beginning and ending class
  - Getting supplies
  - Getting students' attention in class
  - Moving within the classroom
  - Emergency procedures
  - Using technology
  - Working alone, with a partner, or in a group
  - Turning in assignments, homework, and make-up work
  - Listening to teacher directions

SELF-REFLECTION QUESTIONS

Take time to reflect on the questions in Figure 5.2 related to your role as a leader and your support of your new teachers. Your responses in both the strengths and challenges columns should help guide you with implement-ing strategies that will impact your school community. You should be able to chart your journey as the instructional leader as you progress through the year.

Figure 5.2 **Self-Reflection Questions**

Reflection Questions	My Strengths	My Challenges	My Strategies
Have we done a classroom gallery walk?			
Have my new teachers toured the school? Do they know where materials can be found, and have I provided them with the materials to start the first day of school?			
Have I provided classroom supplies to all new teachers?			
Have I checked to make sure that all of the technology is working? If not, have I contacted someone to come and fix it?			
Have I provided time for my new staff to get to know each other and their mentors?			
Have I provided each new teacher with contacts, emergency knowledge, and procedures for beginning the first day?			

Reflection Questions	My Strengths	My Challenges	My Strategies
Have I provided sample opening-of-school activities (by grade level) for the first week of school?			
Have I modeled instructional strategies for my new teachers to use on the first day?			
Have I helped first-year teachers plan their agendas, objectives, and lessons for the first week? Do they have extra activities in case their students finish early?			
What have I forgotten?			
Do my first-year teachers know how to get help?			

Classroom Management

QUOTE

Teaching eighth graders is just about like herding mosquitoes. Once you get one under control, another one just pops up.

—McKinley Johnson, lateral entry
middle-grades science teacher

STORY FROM THE FIELD

A fire in a classroom is never a good thing, but it's especially bad when it is deliberately set by a student. One of my new teachers had the experience of having a sixth-grade student set fire to the papers in the cubbyhole of his desk. At first she was not sure that she was actually seeing smoke and flames, but then the student next to this child started screaming and yelling. The teacher's reaction was a proactive response to the situation. She quickly walked to get the fire extinguisher and put out the fire; then she called for the resource officer, and together they removed the offending student from the classroom. When this happened a second time, the teacher had the other child get the extinguisher, she put out the fire, and she again called for the resource officer. The third time was the charm, as the student was expelled from the school and asked not to return. While some of us may view the intentional setting of a fire as justifying an immediate suspension, this school did not take that action.

We have to commend this teacher for being proactive in this situation. With the return of the student after the first event, she was aware that this might occur again. Her response choice could have gone two ways, and she chose to be calm and composed, allowing her to have total control of the situation. She did not panic, get angry, or raise her voice during the incident. I do not think that she had ever considered this situation could occur, but she knew what to do and how to get help. Her management plan was clearly in place, as she told her students to remain calm and that she would handle each step to ensure their safety. She told me that her students were 100% responsive and followed her directions without confusion or question.

THE ADMINISTRATOR'S ROLE

Classroom management is the number-one concern of all new teachers. They typically do not get to practice these skills and rely on day-to-day trial and error to get their management style implemented so that it works. It is on-the-job training, and no one can entirely prepare a teacher for what to expect in a classroom. It is also one of the top reasons that they leave.

Teachers who learn to manage the classroom keep students on task and actively engaged with their learning. Beginning teachers often feel that inability to manage their classes is a sign of weakness and are often afraid to ask for help. It takes time to develop the skills for managing student behavior, and conversations and demonstrations in this area should be ongoing during the school year. Being overprepared and overplanned for class will reduce the amount of time spent on behavioral issues. What happens on the first day of school determines the pace and success during the rest of the year. Posting the rules, rewards, and consequences provides students with a reminder of the teacher's expectations. It is important to establish a working set of procedures from the beginning so that students understand the way the class will operate. Schools and grade-level teams often develop and implement a consistent behavior management plan that is structured for classroom operation. There is no shortage of information on classroom management!

Defining Classroom Management

Classroom management refers to everything a teacher does to organize time, space, and students so that effective instruction occurs every day. It is a skill to learn how to keep students on task, actively engage them, and manage the logistics of a classroom. Learning to manage a classroom full of students takes time and practice.

Robert Marzano (2003) investigated the effects of various classroom management processes on a number of outcomes, including achievement. His findings indicated that the classrooms of teachers who had strong, positive relationships with students had more student engagement, more behaviors that evidenced students' respect for themselves and others, and fewer behavior issues, and that students in these classrooms showed higher achievement as well.

Rules and Procedures in Your School

We all know that what happens on the first day of school determines what happens during the rest of the year. Helping new teachers understand the difference between rules and procedures is a first step in supporting their classroom management plan. *Rules* are general expectations that guide student behavior, while *procedures* communicate specific expectations for behaviors through an observable process. Your knowledge of your staff will help you guide them in designing rules and procedures that are specific to the both them and their students. Most classrooms will have three to five rules and multiple sets of procedures. Rules should be clear and stated in a positive tone. Several schools that I work with use "I can" statements for establishing procedures in the classroom (see Figure 6.1).

Figure 6.1   Rules and "I Can" Statements

Rules	"I Can" Statements
Be respectful.	I can keep my feet, hands, and objects to myself.
Be prepared every day.	I can bring paper, pencils, books, and homework with me to class.
Listen and speak politely.	I can raise my hand before speaking or asking for help.
Be on time.	I can be in my assigned seat when the bell rings.
Do your best.	I can be ready to learn something new each day.

One of the challenges that new teachers face is the organization and management of their classrooms. Many of them do not know where to begin with establishing a behavior management system that will work for them and their students. As I walk through classrooms on a daily basis, I notice that implementation of procedures becomes a problem. Figure 6.2 on the next page provides several observable behaviors and questions that will guide new teachers in developing a positive behavior model for their classroom.

Rewards

Everyone likes to be rewarded, and everyone hates to be reprimanded. New teachers need to know how to effectively implement both, based on district or school policies. There should be a hierarchy of each, and what you expect in your building depends on clear, fair, and consistent implementation of each. It is imperative that you explain the school's behavior management plan and how it is implemented and supported within the classroom. Self-discipline is taught, not with tangible rewards, but with intrinsic motivation that comes from within a child.

Figure 6.2 Observable Procedures and Questions to Ask New Teachers

Observable Procedures	Questions to Ask New Teachers
Students entering and exiting the classroom	What are your expectations for students entering and exiting the classroom?
Beginning and ending the class period instruction	How do you begin and end class so that students are engaged quickly and leave with a self-assessment completed?
Getting student attention and giving directions	How do you get students' attention when giving directions? How do students get your attention?
Transitions	What techniques do you use to transition from one activity to another or from place to place?
Students getting materials and supplies	How do students know how to get and use materials and supplies?
Individual, pair, and group work	What expectations do you have for work time?

As you observe classrooms, look for ways that the teacher supports rules and procedures. One of the most common problems with new teachers is the lack of consistency and equality for every student in the classroom. There is a great opportunity to help your new teachers grow professionally with specific and timely feedback. The list of rewards should outnumber the list of consequences, as the emphasis should be on the positive rather than the negative. The problem is knowing what each student responds to, and acting on it. One-on-one conferences with students could provide insight into what works for them in changing a behavior pattern.

The following is a list of possible rewards to look for during a classroom visit.

- Verbal praise
- Special recognition (bulletin boards, newsletters, blogs, posters)
- Special classroom jobs (taking care of the class pet, taking up papers, line leader)
- Certificates, ribbons
- Bonus points
- Tangible items
- Positive notes or phone call home
- Choosing work-time music
- Extra computer time
- Raffle entry for end-of-week surprise
- Stickers

- Treat box selections
- Student of the week desk

Consequences

All teachers want their students to be productive and happy in their classroom. Every teacher uses strategies that acknowledge and support appropriate academic and social characteristics in their students. The topic of rewards and consequences is not new to education, and how you help support your new teachers should be a reflection of your district, state, and local policies. Rewards are often used to reduce misbehavior and encourage appropriate behavior, and they must be aligned with student needs.

When students break the rules or procedures, there must be fair and equitable consequences for their behavior. New teachers often are not prepared to develop a series of effective consequences in their classroom. Many of them "fight the little battles" and will send a student out of the room to the office. We have all seen teachers who send students out because of a lack of a pencil, lateness to class, or not having homework. Teachers need to learn to handle problems on their own in cases where students are breaking the classroom rules or not following procedures. When they send a student out, this results in their giving up control, and the student *will* most likely return to that same classroom. The major issue in implementing consequences is consistency and fairness to all. If a teacher tells a student of a consequence but does not follow through, the teacher's credibility is compromised, and this empty threat is meaningless to the student. It is amazing how well students can learn to play the game. However, we must let our new teachers know that there are times when calling for help is the right choice.

It is important for leaders to take the time to discuss rules, procedures, rewards, and consequences with their new teachers. Their behavior plans must be acceptable to you and in compliance with the state, district, and school principles. Monitoring what happens in the classroom and providing time to observe, with feedback, will help your new staff develop their own positive behavior actions.

Intervening to Prevent Failure or Frustration

So what do new teachers do when they need help? Usually nothing, because they are afraid to ask, do not know who to ask, or have no idea that they actually need help. One of the worst questions to ask a new teacher is, "How are you doing?" Their response is typically "fine," and that provides you with no feedback on specific needs and concerns. You should rephrase the question: "What can I do to help you?" Even though they may not know, you can probe deeper and find out if there is something of concern to them. It will be very clear as you visit and observe that they have needs for help with organization, management, or instruction. If you find issues with your new teachers, you need to approach the situation with great respect and convey a sense that you value in their efforts.

Accountability for Positive Behavior

There is a wealth of information that supports the research on positive interventions for behavior. Each teacher must develop a management style that works for her or him, and must practice it with patience and your support. Some will learn how to manage a classroom faster than others. This is an opportunity for you to actually model classroom strategies for effective, positive behavior. There are also situations in which you must explain that immediate help is needed. This includes situations in which students are endangering themselves or others; students are using weapons, drugs, or alcohol; or a school policy that needs additional support. Have you taught first-year staff how to get a rapid response?

Here are seven strategies to share with your new teachers.

- Teach your teachers that it is okay to smile and provide quick positive reinforcement. This could include high-fives, pats on the back, silent cheers, and multiple other fun activities.

- Model the use of teacher voice and the teacher look. Have teachers practice using a change in voice tone (while not yelling) and/or a look for disciplinary effect. I actually gave my new teachers a mirror so they could practice.

- Talk about proximity to students and walking over and standing next to a student who is off task. The idea is to use nonverbal communication while continuing to teach.

- Discuss the instructional zone in the classroom. Teachers all have particular places where they give directions. Make sure your new teachers are consistent with this.

- Develop a plan for positive phone calls, notes, or e-mails. Teachers should base these on their observable procedures in the classroom.

- Make sure teachers call on all students equally. Observe whether there are differences in the number of students called between boys and girls, students in front and back, and students on the right and left sides of the room.

- Hold all students accountable for learning and participating. Use names on cards or craft sticks with names to call on random students during questioning time.

WHAT ELSE CAN I DO?

You need to provide consistency and commitment to helping new teachers learn how to manage a classroom full of students. Knowing where your teachers' strengths and challenges are within this process will give you target areas for celebration and improvement.

Figure 6.3 Establishing Rules and Procedures Checklist

Take time to reflect on how to implement classroom rules and procedures in order to establish the desired student behaviors in your classroom. What are your strengths and challenges in relation to each? Talk with your principal about your need for support.

Do my students know how to . . . ?	Strengths	Challenges
Respond to my rules, procedures, and rewards		
Enter and exit the classroom		
Come prepared with materials and supplies		
Follow tardy-to-class procedures		
Follow directions for specific tasks		
Give attention to me as I provide instruction		
Ask questions and get help		
Get supplies and materials		

(Continued)

Figure 6.3   (Continued)

Do my students know how to . . . ?	Strengths	Challenges
Work individually, in pairs, and in groups		
Move within the classroom		
Respond appropriately to classroom transitions		
Respond appropriately to emergency situations		
Get make-up work and what to do with it		
Turn in work and materials, including classwork and homework		
Request permission to leave the classroom		

- Teach about rules and procedures, and give a generic list of classroom procedures that students should follow. Use the Establishing Rules and Procedures Checklist on pages 81–82 (Figure 6.3) as a guide to help you and your new staff reflect on what is working and what needs improvement.

- Have your new teachers model and share how they will introduce their management plan to their students.

- Talk about the use of positive behavior strategies, such as phone calls to parents and notes for students.

- Video tape several of your great teachers at work, and have your new staff watch and reflect on lesson design. Provide a series of reflection questions to guide their learning.

- Help teachers post their rules and procedures in student-friendly terms.

- Make sure rules, procedures, rewards, and consequences are aligned to the school mission and vision and communicated to parents.

- Follow up on all new teachers' management plans, and spend time supporting the implementation of their classroom procedures.

- Help your new teachers identify the root cause of a behavior issue. Does it stem from a need for attention, anger, nonengagement, noncompliance, or other causes?

- Use your mentors as support, and allow your new teachers to observe master teachers and their management skills.

- Write a letter to the students in the classroom praising them for following the teacher's directions and procedures. It might start with "Dear Ms. __'s students, I am so impressed with. . . ."

- Use your iPad or phone to take pictures of students doing good things. Send the photos to the teacher to share in the classroom as models of what exemplary students look like in their class.

SELF-REFLECTION QUESTIONS

Take time to reflect on the questions in Figure 6.4 related to your role as a leader and your support of your new teachers. Your responses in both the strengths and challenges columns should help guide you with implementing strategies that will impact your school community. You should be able to chart your journey as the instructional leader as you progress through the year.

Figure 6.4 **Self-Reflection Questions**

Reflection Questions	My Strengths	My Challenges	My Strategies
How do I provide my new staff with the schoolwide behavior policies?			
How do I make sure that new teachers have their rules, consequences, procedures, and rewards posted in their room?			
How do I provide practice for my teachers to deal with crises and issues?			
Have I talked about and modeled the codes used in emergency situations?			
Have I helped my new teachers with parent conferences and documentation of student behavior?			

Reflection Questions	My Strengths	My Challenges	My Strategies
How do I monitor my new teachers' progress in developing a classroom management plan?			
Have I allowed my new staff to observe other teachers who have exemplary management skills?			
How do we, as a school, support positive behavior?			
How do I help new teachers with behavioral interventions? What have they tried?			
How do I know if one of my new teachers is in trouble with management and/or is inconsistent in implementation of her or his plan?			

Curriculum Standards and Planning

QUOTE

What do we want our students to know? How do we know they are learning? How do we help them to move forward?

—Fourth-grade team

STORY FROM THE FIELD

My junior high principal called all of the science teachers into his office one summer and told us that we would be teaching additional classes. Since I was the youngest on the staff, it seemed like all the good choices were taken and when it came to me, I didn't know what to select. He reminded me that I was from Florida so I could teach oceanography despite the fact that we had no textbook or curriculum. The first day of class presented me with 60 students and nothing to teach, so I asked them what they wanted to know about the ocean and listed their answers on chart paper. Day 2 was all about what questions they had about the ocean, and on Day 3, I collected input about how they would like to learn this information. This set the stage for me to write a semester-long course that integrated the sciences with language arts, math, history, and cultural arts. All of this turned into a master's thesis, which included a set of teaching modules related to the Outer Banks of North Carolina. In addition to teaching earth science and math, I taught oceanography for 15 years; my classes included week-long coastal field trips and a curriculum that was engaging, motivating, and appropriate for all students.

Some of us remember the day when we had no standards, curriculum guides, or assessment-driven accountability. It was actually fun to teach, but inconsistency was common across the district and among schools, and transient students were taught a mixed selection of curriculum based on varying core content standards. With the standards movement beginning in the 1990s in North Carolina, we all had mixed feelings as to the impact that this would have on our teaching and learning. Mandated programs came and went, students were tested, and teachers were held accountable for teaching a set of standards that were new and different. As we reflect on the implementation of new standards today, we must provide a systematic process for our teachers to use to learn and implement the new standards.

THE ADMINISTRATOR'S ROLE

Imagine a middle school in need of help to improve the quality of instruction and assessment. As the building principal, what would the label "school in crisis" mean to you and the school community? Here's a typical scenario: Morale is extremely low, and teachers are frustrated at not being able to move the students forward in learning. Every teacher is struggling with the standards and how to use the district-provided data to inform their instructional decisions. Numerous district initiatives and programs have been mandated over the past 10 years, and improvement results have not been quick enough for district leaders. This scenario is true in so many schools around the country. Teachers are trying to implement too many programs at the same time, while not giving any of them time to make a difference.

As the instructional leader, you must make decisions to move forward with a systematic process for improving teaching and learning. It needs to be simple, easy to implement, and 100% teacher–student centered. The focus must be on a model that allows dedicated time for both horizontal and vertical alignment with grade-level collaboration and communication. All administrators are now called the "instructional leader" for their school.

The Common Core State Standards Initiative (CCSSI), coordinated by the Council of Chief State School Officers (CCSSO) and the National Governors Association Center for Best Practices (NGA Center), released the Common Core State Standards (CCSS) for English language arts (ELA) and mathematics in June of 2010. The Next Generation Science Standards (NGSS) were released in April of 2013. Whether a state has adopted the Common Core or the Next Generation Science Standards is not the issue.

The accountability imposed on schools requires that all students demonstrate proficiency in reading and math. For beginning teachers, the decision of what to teach, when to teach it, and how to engage students in learning is a task that they face on a daily basis, especially when they are trying to learn so many other skills and strategies at the same time.

The transition to the Common Core and the Next Generation Science Standards will require teachers to develop and expand on a new set of skills in anticipation of preparing students for a more rigorous and demanding education. Veteran teachers will have to shift how they teach, and assess and redesign their teacher-directed instruction to more student-centered learning. This will be a challenge for all teachers.

One of my principals and I were visiting classrooms and were sitting in the back of an eighth-grade algebra class. The first-year teacher was modeling how to solve an equation on the board. Students were very compliant and copying the process in their notebooks for future reference. All of a sudden, the principal and I looked at each other and realized that the teacher was doing the problem incorrectly. Students had no idea that he was giving them wrong information.

Everyone knows that subject matter knowledge and how to teach are integral components of what teachers need to be able to do in a classroom. Quality teaching involves teachers challenging their students to solve problems, having high expectations, monitoring and reflecting on their teaching, and teaching the language and love of their subject area. To meet the needs of teachers, we must provide opportunities for them to deepen their content knowledge and learn the methods of teaching. Identifying the new teachers who have a college degree but not educational experience will help determine the type of support needed. One of my new math teachers said,

> I am a math major and know how to do math. The problem was that I didn't know how to teach it to algebra students who really didn't want to learn about algebra.

A Strategic Planning Model

The phrase *strategic planning* originates in warfare. The word *strategy* comes from the Greek word *strategos*, which is a combination of *stratos* (army) and *adein* (to conduct). We have all heard the phrase, "You can plan to fail or you can fail to plan." In the case of working with new teachers and schools, it is a case of both. We have to develop a consistent, teacher-friendly format for articulating the instructional process in the classroom.

When I was the assistant to the regional superintendent and in charge of the curriculum, instruction, and assessments in 21 priority schools in the Charlotte-Mecklenburg School System, the first step was to observe in every new teacher's classroom in the schools in Region B. My job was to identify the strengths and challenges that I saw would impact teaching and student learning. Despite the numerous obstacles that new teachers faced, enthusiasm and willingness to success overpowered any challenge. They wanted to learn and learn quickly. The *stratego,* or civil-military officials elected by the citizens of Athens, were charged with the expectation that they would prepare and implement plans in order to win wars and battles. This is no different that the daily workings in a classroom.

The United States began using this term in the late 1970s and early 1980s. I can remember being given a handbook entitled *Strategic School Improvement Plan* that all of us were to follow and use in our daily teaching. It was the least teacher-friendly piece of text I had ever read. At no time did it talk about the students and where they were and where they needed to be. Nor did it differentiate at all among the extreme variety of individual school populations. It was clearly a district initiative, which was passed on to the administration and then to us as the end-all to school-based reform for the future.

Effective teaching should begin with a systematic process that guides grade-level teams through the planning of quality units of study and engaging lessons. There is not a shortage of curriculum material, but the problem is just what to do with it all. To help teachers understand the process of planning, we must transition from an individual "this is my classroom" approach to work with professional learning teams.

There are multiple educators in the field who have developed models for instructional planning, including Grant Wiggins and Jay McTighe (*Understanding by Design,* 2005) and Larry Ainsworth (*Rigorous Curriculum Design,* 2001), as well as me (*Five Easy Steps to a Balanced Science Program,* 2010). All of the models have student learning in common, and each has three guiding questions:

- What should be taught?
- How should it be taught?
- How should learning be assessed?

The Strategic Planning Process

Today, we think of strategic planning as having two components: (1) thinking big, considering all options and anticipating any changes, and (2) focusing on clear, concise long-term goals and objectives. When we want to think big, we should also think out of the box. What we have done in the past, for many schools, has not provided the changes we need to improve teaching and learning. Many administrators tell me that they are just "stuck in the middle" and have too many distractions that take away from the time they should be spending with teachers.

I was asked by several principals to help teachers implement a strategic planning process for their middle schools. To tackle the issues of instruction, I suggested a series of three steps that would give grade-level educators a process for unit development that would align their instruction and assessment with the standards. We began looking at the standards, analyzing current student test data, assessing instructional presentations, and deciding on a model that would be teacher-friendly and work for all content and grade levels. The empty workroom was turned into the strategic planning center, where grade-level content teams could meet weekly to discuss progress in implementing the standards-based curriculum. Large posters, representing each grade and content, were put up on the walls. Standards for the quarter were paced out along with the aligned objective, instructional strategy, and assessment. Current test data were displayed along with a target goal for improvement. For example, eighth-grade algebra scores were showing that students were 27% proficient at the beginning of the year. The goal for the end of first quarter was 50%, which represented what they called SMART goals (specific, measurable, accurate, relevant, and timely). As each quarter ended, results were added to the posters, so progress could be charted and shared. Students were made aware of where they were, where they needed to be, and what strategies would take them there. In addition, the master schedule was revised so that 45 minutes were allocated at the beginning of the day for remediation or enrichment.

Each team of teachers decided to follow three steps in designing their units of study for each quarter. The posters reflected a visual image that was vertically and horizontally aligned by grade level. Everyone in the building followed the same process during the year.

Step 1: Identify what to teach.

As administrators become more familiar with the new standards, the opportunity exists to help all teachers gain a better understanding of what the standards mean and how to implement them across K–12 classrooms. This first step takes teachers through the identification of their grade-level standards. Included in this step is the "unpacking" or "deconstructing" of the standards and identification of the skills and content that students need to know in order to be proficient at grade level. Learning concepts and guiding questions are written to help teachers plan and monitor their instruction and student understanding. Key vocabulary terms are listed in tiers based on the population of students in the school.

Figure 7.1 shows a template for planning a unit of study for any content.

Figure 7.2 gives an example of how the template could be used, in this case with the Next Generation Science Standards—High School Life Science.

Step 2: Identify how to teach.

Once the standards have been identified and we know what to teach, we need to focus on the instructional practices within the classroom. This is an area where new teachers may need a lot of support and guidance from you and your master teachers. Research from Robert Marzano (Marzano, Pickering, & Pollock, 2001) and John Hattie (2009) supports best instructional practices in the classroom. If learning is to occur, the teacher must have a variety of teaching strategies to implement with a diverse population of students.

Figure 7.1 Template for Planning a Unit of Study

Standard(s)			
These are the actual standards taken from the document.			
What students will do	**What students will know**	**Bloom's Taxonomy**	**Webb's Depth of Knowledge**
These are the skills—usually verbs that indicate what the students will do to show mastery of the standard.	This is the content—usually nouns that represent the core learning of the standard.	This represents the six levels of cognitive thinking in the standard. 1. Remember 2. Understand 3. Apply 4. Analyze 5. Evaluate 6. Create	This represents the holistic level of thinking of the standard. There are four levels: 1. Recall and Reproduction 2. Skills and Concepts 3. Strategic Thinking 4. Extended Thinking

Learning Concept
The learning concepts represent the big understandings that are the foundation of what we want students to discover by the end of the unit.

Guiding Questions
Guiding questions engage and motivate student learning. They are posted in the classroom as a guide that influences student thinking and learning.

Key Vocabulary		
Tier 1	**Tier 2**	**Tier 3**
Tier 1 represents the actual terminology found written in the standards.	Tier 2 vocabulary includes words that cross other content areas.	Tier 3 vocabulary represents content-specific terminology that is used only with this content.

Figure 7.2 Sample Template for a Science Unit of Study

NGSS Performance Expectation	HS-LS1–3
	Plan and conduct an investigation to provide evidence that feedback mechanisms maintain homeostasis.

What students will do

What students will know

Plan and conduct	An investigation
To provide	Evidence that feedback mechanisms maintain homeostasis

Learning Concept

Guiding Questions

1. Structure determines function.	1. How are structures and function related?
2. The body is a system of multiple interacting subsystems.	2. How does the human body maintain its structure and function?

Key Vocabulary

Tier 1	Tier 2	Tier 3
Structure	Feedback	Heart rate
Function	Cell	Homeostasis
Data	Response	Stomata
Moisture	Stimulus	Feedback mechanisms
Temperature	Hierarchical	
	Interaction	
	System	
	Tissue	
	Organs	

Source: Next Generation Science Standards, www.nextgenscience.org

The template in Figure 7.3 provides suggestions that apply to students at all grade levels. Reflect on activities that you could model for your new teachers.

Step 3: Identify how to assess.

Assessment is the process of gathering data about teaching and learning. The data provide a snapshot of what students know and don't know for the purpose of evaluating student performance. Decisions about next steps are based on an analysis of the data. Black and Wiliam (2009) have demonstrated the importance of formative assessments that can lead to feedback during learning. They write, "Practice in a classroom is formative to the extent that evidence about student achievement is elicited, interpreted, and used by teachers to make decisions about the next steps in instruction" (p. 29). Based on their work in schools, Leahy and Wiliam (2009) state,

> When formative assessment practices are integrated into the minute-to-minute and day-to-day classroom activities of teachers, substantial increases in student achievement of the order of a 70–80 percent increase in the speed of learning—are possible, even when the outcomes are measured with externally mandated standardized tests. (as quoted in Hattie, 2009, p. 128)

The focus on assessment *for* learning rather than assessment *of* learning has gained national attention over the past years. Classrooms where assessment for learning is practiced have students who are active in their personal learning and growth. Assessment for learning enables teachers to

- plan and modify their teaching activities for individuals, groups, or the class.
- identify student strengths and challenges.
- provide students with feedback that guides their learning progressions.
- allow for self-reflection and progress monitoring.
- use a variety of assessment tools to determine student learning needs.

Figure 7.4 suggests ways in which you can support your new teachers with these types of assessments.

Lesson Planning

Imagine a kindergarten classroom abuzz with excitement. The students have a variety of items including a marble, marshmallow, cracker, metal screw, and a raisin. They have completed the science standard on making observations and building an understanding of the properties of common objects. The "sink or float" assessment will allow them to demonstrate what they have learned. The teacher has provided a lab response sheet, so

Figure 7.3   **Instructional Practices**

Instructional Practices		
	Classroom Suggestions	**Suggested Teacher-Directed and Student-Centered Activities**
Research-based instructional practices for all students*	❑ Identifying similarities and differences ❑ Summarizing and note taking ❑ Reinforcing effort, providing recognition ❑ Homework and practice ❑ Nonlinguistic representations ❑ Cooperative learning ❑ Setting objectives, providing feedback ❑ Generating and testing hypotheses ❑ Cues, questions, and advance organizers	
Differentiation for advanced learners	❑ Tiered lessons ❑ Compacting ❑ Learning centers ❑ Advanced text ❑ Leveled groups	
Special education modifications	❑ IEPs ❑ Anecdotal notes ❑ Cooperative grouping ❑ Teacher read aloud ❑ Hands-on inquiry activities ❑ Teacher demonstrations ❑ Visuals and video ❑ Interactive notes with visuals ❑ Leveled reading materials	
English language learners	❑ Cooperative groups—teacher groups students strategically ❑ Partner pair and group reading and talk/collaboration ❑ Multiple opportunities to speak ❑ Teacher reads and models ❑ Hands-on inquiry activities ❑ Teacher demonstrations	

*Adapted from Marzano et al., 2001

Figure 7.4 **Types of Assessments**

Type of Assessment	Description	Suggested Formats
Diagnostic assessment	This type of assessment provides teachers with information about students' prior knowledge, so they know where students are and where they need to go with their learning.	❑ Pretest ❑ Self-reflection ❑ Conferencing ❑ Technology-based assessment
Formative assessment	This type of assessment occurs during the instruction time and allows teachers to identify student progress based on their teaching. Formative assessment can be informal or formal, but the purpose is to guide instruction to meet the needs of the students. Results of formative assessment provide quick feedback to the teacher and students. This is the most powerful form of assessment for helping teachers improve student achievement.	❑ Teacher observation ❑ Short quiz ❑ Thumbs up/down ❑ Homework ❑ Enter and exit slips ❑ Writing prompts ❑ Peer feedback ❑ Reflection journals ❑ Response logs ❑ Formats may include selected-response items such as multiple choice, true-false, matching, or fill-in-the-blank and constructed-response items, such as short answer or extended response.
Summative assessment	This type of assessment takes places at the end of a unit, and the results are used to compare classes or schools within a district. There is often a delay in getting results, because it takes time to score and return these assessments to students. But these results can help inform improvements for the next year.	❑ SAT ❑ ACT ❑ NAEP ❑ Teacher-designed unit assessments ❑ Performance assessments ❑ Portfolios ❑ Long-term projects

students can record their observations for each item. This science instruction is designed around conceptual understanding and performance assessments. Behavioral observations, written work, and performance tasks are used to assess what students know and are able to do.

I was very involved in helping the teacher of this class understand the new science standards and the impact that these would have on teaching and learning. It is important that everyone talks about how to help support and guide the learning of both the teacher and the students.

Daily Instructional Planning

Grade-level strategic planning allows teachers to identify the standards and objectives that must be taught and the process to organize each within an identified timeline. Once the units of study are scheduled into a year-long pacing calendar, strategies for effectively teaching the standards can be incorporated into daily lesson plans. Lesson plans serve as a roadmap for understanding what students will do and learn during the lesson. Numerous formats for lesson design are available, but all contain components to help make learning meaningful and purposeful. The terminology may vary, but the components usually include a focus or anticipatory set, stated objective, teacher input, modeling, guided practice with checking for understanding, independent practice, and summarizing of new knowledge.

We know that planning is an essential tool for effective instruction in the classroom. This is one area where new teachers struggle, and providing specific examples of lesson plans, based on a template, will help them learn to put the pieces of a daily lesson together. It takes time to learn to plan a daily or weekly set of lessons. Teachers must reflect on what worked, what didn't, and how to change the outcomes, but they need to know how to recognize each of these pieces. A solid planning process is integral to a teacher's efforts in identifying appropriate curriculum, instructional strategies, and resources to address the needs of all students. Planning includes the content of the lesson, materials and resources, teaching strategies, and assessment—all in a well-paced amount of time.

WHAT ELSE CAN I DO?

Dr. Lynnice Carter, assistant superintendent of the Pontotoc County School District in Mississippi, supports a unique learning opportunity for new staff members. Four times a year, they come together to participate in a book study using Todd Whitaker's *What Great Teachers Do Differently* (2011). Teachers are assigned a chapter to read and/or a video to watch and then to report on their learning back in their buildings. It provides them a chance to reflect on what they are doing well and on areas that may need growth and improvement. In addition to these book talks, everyone in the central office adopts a new teacher for the year. They serve as mentors, visit classrooms, provide feedback, and help new teachers learn the skills and knowledge needed to make it through the first year.

You need to provide consistency and commitment in helping new teachers with yearly and daily planning. A systematic process, led by you, defines what students know prior to instruction, during it, and after instruction has taken place. Knowing where your teachers' strengths and challenges are within this process will give you target areas for celebration and improvement.

- Teach them to identify the skills and content within the standards.

- Provide time for all teachers to meet and share content knowledge and teaching strategies.

- Provide "tutoring" sessions so that new teachers can practice the content before presenting it.

- Provide exemplars of lesson plans, and talk about the components that make a good instructional presentation.

- Monitor and provide feedback on their lesson plans.

- Model and practice teacher-directed and student-centered strategies to use with students. Integrate these into your staff meetings so all can benefit.

- Show all teachers how to integrate reading, writing, and vocabulary into their grade-level content areas.

- Provide time for your new teachers to meet with and observe their mentors and other master teachers.

- Provide a classroom timer for lesson pacing.

- Develop a set of questions for new teachers to ask their students, such as "What are you learning?" "Where do you need to work more?" and "What is the outcome of your learning?"

- Through detailed lesson plans, create a schedule for reviewing the use of standards and objectives in daily instructional presentations.

- Place the grade-level strategic planning calendars in a location for other teachers to observe and integrate content topics.

- Help your teachers work backward, using data and goal-setting as the beginning point of unit and lesson design.

SELF-REFLECTION QUESTIONS

Take time to reflect on the questions in Figure 7.5 related to your role as a leader and your support of your new teachers. Your responses in both the strengths and challenges columns should help guide you with implementing strategies that will impact your school community. You should be able to chart your journey as the instructional leader as you progress through the year.

Figure 7.5   **Self-Reflection Questions**

Reflection Questions	My Strengths	My Challenges	My Strategies
How do I explain the importance of team planning and collaboration for learning the content standards?			
How do I share our systematic planning process for long- and short-term goals?			
How do I share my knowledge of the standards with my grade-level teams?			
What data are the most critical to use for guiding student achievement improvement? Where is the school the strongest and the weakest?			
How do I determine the best location and times for team planning?			
Have I created uninterrupted instructional planning time for my teams?			

(Continued)

Figure 7.5 (Continued)

Reflection Questions	My Strengths	My Challenges	My Strategies
How do I share lesson planning? Did I provide exemplars for my new teachers to see and understand?			
How have I monitored my new teachers' lesson plans and provided feedback for each?			
What has been my role in team meetings?			
How do I hold each team accountable for its planning?			
What additional personnel have I used to help support planning?			

Collaboration and Communication

Dream big! We are where choices become opportunities.

—Jack Baldermann, principal

STORY FROM THE FIELD

Jack Baldermann comes to school every day totally fired up for his job. His multitude of experiences provides him with a wealth of skills and knowledge that he openly shares with his school community. He has been a principal for more than 20 years but has a renewed sense of excitement and accomplishment after being at Westmont High School for the past three years. His passion for people and what he does is very clear through his voice and actions. Two years ago, the school had a graduation rate of 88%, which was the state average. Today, it is the most improved school in Illinois, with a 99% graduation rate. The idea is that the staff will do whatever it takes to make a difference, using a philosophy that there is no excuse or circumstance they can't tackle. Baldermann's first month in the building was a time for listening and collecting information. He and his staff began developing a new philosophy for success, establishing goals and interventions, and communicating openly with students, parents, and the board of education.

THE ADMINISTRATOR'S ROLE

Westmont High School is a Title I school; 40% of its students qualify for free or reduced-price lunch. The 450 students and staff all know each other, work hard, and celebrate success. This past year, the school was in the top 1% in the nation and had the most improved advanced placement program in Illinois, along with the best test scores in school history. Reading and math scores jumped significantly, ACT exam scores had double digit gains, and morale was at an all-time high. Suspension rates dropped, and enrollment in advanced placement (AP) courses rose. Where last year only three students passed their AP exams, this year, 140 students passed.

I had the opportunity to learn about Mr. Baldermann from one of his teachers at the Illinois Reading Conference in 2014. She could not stop talking about how wonderful he was and how lucky she was to be at Westmont. This was her second year at the school, and although she was not new to teaching, she was absolutely sold on the vision, mission, and philosophy that he brought to this school.

This is a school where the principal is the instructional leader and promotes innovation, risk taking, and transformation through collaboration and communication. Structures and processes are in place for all teachers to have time to discuss, review, and revise the methods and strategies that make a difference in learning for all students.

Expectations that all students will learn and succeed are embedded in every thought process. Staff don't just *say* that all children can learn; they have an internal belief that they can actually make it happen. At assemblies every other Friday, students and teachers are recognized for their accomplishments, and goals are revisited and shared. Learning and improvement never stops at Westmont High School.

Communication in Teacher-Led Teams

At Mineral Springs Elementary School, principal Debra Gladstone allocates time each month to meet with her new staff members and provide support based on her conversations and observations in their classrooms. She asks about their successes while giving professional development support. The focus for her teachers is on improving classroom management and reading instruction to improve student achievement. Her philosophy is that everyone has room to grow and improve, and knowing the needs of her teachers allows her to work with them to develop appropriate learning experiences.

Communication within teams of teachers is one of the correlates of effective schools. In 1995, Linda Darling-Hammond and Milbrey McLaughlin wrote about the habits and cultures inside a school and the relationships between these and teaching practices and student achievement. Time to discuss and have a deep analysis of what is working and what is not is crucial to school improvement. Collaboration on goals, data analysis, common formative assessments, and best instructional practices drives the decision-making process in schools. Teachers who rely on a collective method for analyzing and interpreting data learn how effective they are at teaching. Discussions about teacher actions are the key to making changes in student achievement. The primary purpose of collaboration is to improve student achievement. Research from Borko (2004) indicates that when teachers collaborate to develop and answer questions informed by data from their own students, their knowledge grows and their practices change.

Collaboration time in schools is defined as a time when educators plan and work together for the benefit of all students. This collaboration does not occur naturally and often is forced upon a teaching staff. With the introduction of professional learning teams and structured planning time, teachers no longer work in isolation. It is imperative that they have time to talk with their colleagues, mentors, and peers to determine what their successes and challenges are with their students. The 2012 MetLife Teacher Survey states that more than 6 in 10 teachers say that time to collaborate with other teachers has decreased or stayed the same in 2012 compared with 2011. With new standards, new methodologies, and new assessments, it is critical that we allow protected time for planning and collaboration. It is interesting to note that when new teachers need advice or help, they will often go to another new teacher and not a more experienced colleague or the principal.

Professional learning communities, where groups of educators work together to analyze and improve teaching behaviors, are common in schools today. This engagement involves an ongoing cycle of questions that encourage deeper team learning and practices. They are the cornerstone of school improvement. Grade-level planning teams should focus on three specific questions centered on an analysis of formative and summative data:

1. What do our students need to know and be able to do when they have completed this grade level?

2. What instructional best practices are we implementing so that all students learn?

3. How do we know what we are doing is working, and what changes do we need to make?

Building a Culture of Collaboration

As we look at building collaboration schools, there are two areas that should be addressed: (1) What does a collaborative culture look like in our building, and (2) how do we create a positive collaborative culture? One of the basic premises is that everyone in the building should believe that all children can and will learn. Discussions around teacher efficacy and the impact that each teacher has on student learning will give you a better understanding of the beliefs and principles that guide your educators' practice.

Every school has a culture and climate. They are obvious from the first moment you walk in the door, enter the front office, and move about the building. Effective schools have teachers who work together through discussion and problem solving for the benefit of their students. School culture is complex and involves values, beliefs, traditions, and history. It is established over time but can be destroyed within weeks if poor leadership comes into place. The actions within and outside the building form the backbone by which the school community is judged and evaluated.

Effective teams share a sense of responsibility for each team meeting and participate equally in the planning and outcomes. Figure 8.1 lists some of the actions they take. As you look at the figure, think about whether you have shared your expectations for the team actions and clearly defined what each looks like for your effective teams.

Developing a Culture for Teaming

Teams are improved when the school leadership provides a set of professional standards that guide the expectations for leadership teams. Resources such as the Council of Chief State School Officers's *Performance Expectations and Indicators for Education Leaders* (Sanders & Kearney, 2008) and Learning Forward's *Standards for Professional Learning* (2011) are excellent resources for creating solid teams. When the principal outlines and shares the expectations for climate, professionalism, communication, and decision making, school achievement is increased. The benefit of collaborative teams is based on three questions:

1. Do your teachers know their strengths and challenges? Have they shared these?

2. Do your teachers know their content, and do they have the skills to implement student-centered instruction?

3. Does everyone know the purpose and outcomes for the team?

Collaborative teaming is defined as two or more people working toward a common goal. Exemplary teams do not develop in isolation, and it takes time and a deep commitment to develop teams of educators that practice intentional communication and ongoing collaboration. In *School Leadership that Works: From Research to Results*, Robert Marzano, Timothy Waters, and Brian McNulty (2005) state that in order to improve student achievement, the leadership must be knowledgeable, highly skilled, and focused on a vision and mission.

One of the best ways to begin establishing a culture of teaming and collaboration is to develop a set of norms that will guide the team's actions. Many principals will allow a team to brainstorm what the expectations for meetings will be and then create a poster or chart that is available at each meeting. Some teams actually verbalize these norms before beginning their work.

Figure 8.1   **Team Actions and Desired Results**

Team Actions	Desired Results
Follow a set of standards for professional development, such as Learning Forward.	
Create a focused agenda, including a review of minutes from previous meeting and summary of previous goals.	
Establish norms, codes of ethics, and roles and responsibilities that are clearly defined.	
Design and prepare instructional materials.	
Collect and provide data and student work analysis.	
Establish SMART goals that are realistic, achievable, and aligned with student needs.	

(Continued)

Figure 8.1 **(Continued)**

Team Actions	Desired Results
Encourage risk taking and problem solving that involve teacher-action research plans.	
Write differentiated learning activities.	
Research best practices to provide for collaborative learning.	
Provide mini in-service sessions on strategies.	
Observe each other and provide feedback; then share with the team.	
Celebrate success on achieved goals.	

Sample norms may include the following:

- Start and end on time.
- Respect ideas from others.
- Listen to all that is suggested before responding.
- Participate fully and equally.
- Stay on task and focused on the purpose.
- Be positive.
- Share roles and responsibilities.

In addition to the norms, some teams assign roles to each team member so that consistency in the work product is established. Similar to the cooperative learning roles, these responsibilities ensure that the work is completed during the designated meeting time.

Sample roles may include those listed in Figure 8.2.

Use Figure 8.3 to monitor your team actions during planning and meetings.

Data in Today's Schools

There is no lack of data in today's schools. The problem is what to do with them, how to use them effectively, and how to plan once we figure them all out. We know the following:

- Schools must foster collaboration and communication.
- Student achievement is everyone's job, and all must be held accountable for what happens in the building.
- There must be a systematic and structured process for meeting time.
- Meeting time must be protected and uninterrupted.
- Norms, roles, and responsibilities must be clearly defined.
- Teaching and learning should be visible to all.
- Data must be collected and analyzed for strengths and weaknesses.
- Needs must be prioritized based on the data, and staff must question the results and determine solutions.
- Goals must be established that are specific, measurable, attainable, relevant, and timely (SMART).
- Research-based instructional practices must be selected, implemented, and reviewed.
- Results must be monitored and changes made based on student impact.

Figure 8.2 **Team Roles and Responsibilities**

Role	Responsibility
Timekeeper	Develops the agenda and distributes it to the team prior to meeting Ensures that the team adheres to the time period and tasks—meeting starts and ends on time Ensures the agenda is followed
Facilitator	Keeps the conversations on point and takes a leadership role in communicating to other stakeholders through webinars, e-mails, or other forms of communication Makes sure all people are heard Keeps team focused on the goal
Data Collector	Provides current student data based on formative assessments, so instructional decisions are timely and relevant Collects and distributes data prior to meeting
Resource Collector	Finds resources and materials that will support the standards, instructional methods, and assessments
Recorder and Note-Taker	Takes copious notes and shares them through electronic means Provides updates to the administration Posts minutes and agenda items in a shared data folder Maintains accurate records in a timely manner
Norms Manager	Reminds team of the norms at the beginning of each meeting, reminds the group of the norms while they are working (if needed), and helps the group to reflect at the end of each meeting on their adherence to the norms
Visual Director	Uses charts and graphic organizers to organize the team's thoughts and processes
The Food Coordinator	Develops a plan for providing and supplying snacks and goodies for the team meeting

Imagine sitting in on a meeting at Westmont High School during planning time. New and veteran teachers come together to talk about students and instruction. Norms are reviewed, goals are revisited, and the discussion begins. Everyone contributes to the conversation around one of three SMART goals at Westmont. These include the graduation rate, advanced placement scores and enrollment numbers, and improvement on the ACT exam for reading, math, and science. The work that the administration and teachers did was outstanding and resulted in the school being the most improved high school in Illinois in 2014.

Westmont High School was recognized on two of the oldest national ranking systems: the *Washington Post* challenge index and in the *U.S. News and World Report* performance indicators among schools.

Figure 8.3 **Team Observation Components**

Team Observation Components	Things to Consider	Observed Results	Observed Challenges
Team Member Behavior	Entering and exiting the room, on-time arrival, verbal and nonverbal communication, voice tones, eye contact, listening, contributions by all, team members seated in a circle		
Team Meetings	Starting/ending on time, agendas, minutes from previous meeting, data collected, statement of purpose, revisit of SMART goals, comfortable location, materials ready		
Roles and Responsibilities	Sense of purpose for each, review of each prior to starting the meeting		
Participation	Contributions by all, discussion and participation by everyone, sharing ideas and suggestions is the norm; start of meeting is not delayed for late attendees		

(Continued)

Figure 8.3 **(Continued)**

Team Observation Components	Things to Consider	Observed Results	Observed Challenges
Decision Making and Problem Solving	Use of consensus, sense of ownership, brainstorming in place, questions posed		
Conflict Resolution	Speakers begin with positive comments, differences are welcomed, open conversations, no side comments		
Team Effectiveness	Shared ownership and leadership, goals met, meeting notes are summarized, there is an element of fun and celebration		

Their accomplishments included the following:

- A 99% graduation rate (up from 88% in 2012, 94% in 2013, and a 10-year average of 90.5%).

- An increase in the number of advanced placement scholars from 3 in 2013 to 16 in 2014.

- An increase in the number of students passing the advanced placement exams (from 29 in 2013 to 140 in 2014).

- Double-digit increases in reading, math, and science scores from 2012 to 2014 on the state-mandated No Child Left Behind exam, which included the ACT.

- An increase in reading scores from a meets/exceeds percentage pass rate of 55% (2012) to 77% (2014). The interactive report of the Illinois State Board of Education shows that Westmont High School outperformed almost every Title 1 school in Illinois except for the select enrollment schools.

- A decrease in out-of-school suspensions; they dropped from 140 in 2012 to 20 in 2014.

The school attributes this growth and success to a strong support system that was based on collaboration and communication. Everyone in the building took ownership for *all* students. Their "no excuses" philosophy and consistent implementation of high expectations were known and practiced by all. A focus on a rigorous, student-centered, high school curriculum; the development and analysis of common formative assessments; and intense concentration on a few SMART goals allowed them to be recognized in the top 1% for regular Title I high schools in Illinois.

The Use of Technology for Communication and Collaboration

Technology is changing the way we teach, learn, and communicate. There is an abundance of tools, and how to use the various devices in the classroom is a topic of great interest. Digital media play an important role in today's schools with students; in many cases the students are more knowledgeable than the teachers about the use of digital media. With the constant changes in the way we incorporate the tools of technology, it is up to all of us to be aware of the innovations and advancements in using social media in the classroom. The benefit is that we are able to connect with school community members by providing real-time information on teaching, student achievements, athletic competitions, meetings, current events, and conditions within the school.

Leaders must also help their new teachers understand the school's online safety and accessibility policies regulating the use of any type of device or media service. There must also be monitoring of usage, and parent permission forms must be kept current and on file for each student.

The other thing to remember is that these devices break, and teachers should have a backup plan so that instruction is not interrupted when they do.

Social media are changing the way we do professional development in that school leaders can establish specific learning networks based on needs and interests. Professional learning teams are using Twitter, Facebook, Google Docs, digital discussion forums, ASCD Edge, and edWeb.net to make connections with other educators. As leaders, I suggest you determine the goal for using social media and create a plan on how to effectively use these tools. Time to learn how to use these should be included in your school improvement plans.

Principal Jay Posick at Merton Intermediate School uses social media to inform his staff of the latest and greatest things happening in and around his school. During the year, he links schoolwide events to Twitter and celebrates the accomplishments going on in his school community. He produces a *Nuts and Bolts* newsletter that provides current information related to teaching and learning. This includes a brief opening paragraph, calendar updates, supporting ideas, quotes, and Internet resources that will help teachers improve their instruction. This week he included quotes from Martin Luther King Jr. and Maya Angelou plus links to celebrate the good things that are taking place in his school to encourage student and teacher learning. He integrates his annual one-word challenge (this year his word was *focus*) into his messages. His ability to provide positive communication is clear in this excerpt from one of his newsletters:

Nuts and Bolts

1.30.15

As we continue our journey together this school year, I just wanted to mention a few things that really stand out to me about you all.

- You are all really putting forth a great effort to develop strong relationships with our students. They may not notice or recognize this, but I sure do.

- You are all working hard to develop as teams to meet the needs of our students, often giving freely of your time during preps and before and after school. The students and families may not notice or recognize this, but I sure do.

- I am really enjoying getting to know each of you better as a teacher as I visit classes more frequently. Now that MAP testing is done for the winter, I'll be in your classes even more frequently. I notice what you are doing to engage our students every day, the effort you put into planning lessons, and the conversations you have with one another and with me.

So what's with this introduction today? As I am doing a book study for "Thanks for the Feedback" on Voxer, I realize that feedback is a necessary evil for all of us. Sometimes we take negative feedback well and sometimes we don't. As educators, I really don't think any of us take positive feedback well. But we should. We should celebrate each others' accomplishments more often. In less than two weeks, at our next RtI Wednesday,

I'll need 10 minutes of your time again for a little activity. No need to prepare anything, but you better bring a writing utensil that can be used on paper.

"We delight in the beauty of the butterfly, but rarely admit the changes it has gone through to achieve that beauty."

—Maya Angelou, American writer

Powerful quotes from Anne Frank (via Flipboard)

#BookLove (via @TonySinanis—Great resources for helping kids find books)

@mertonint on Twitter

#mertonint on Twitter

#mustangU on Twitter

Family s'more for 1.30.15

I hope that you were able to relax today in your fitness gear. Sometimes it's just nice to relax at school after a long week. I am looking forward to spending a great deal of time in classes today and then again all next week. With MAP testing finished for the Winter, my focus (my #oneword for the year) is now on you and the students. I refocus with a "no office day" today. I'll be doing mini-observations, talking with students, and joining in on as many learning experiences as possible. If you can, join the students and I for lunch and recess. All of us moving together on Fitness Day would be awesome! So my focus returns to supporting you as educators, reconnecting with our students, and being thankful for the opportunities I have each and every day learning with you. How is your #oneword going so far this year?

Have a great weekend!

Jay

BEST

Believe, **E**ncourage, **S**hare, **T**rust

Mr. Posick—and every leader featured in this book—use some type of social media to communicate with teachers, students, and the school community. As I have talked with all of them, I have noticed they all suggest beginning slowly and learning how to use the multitude of resources and tools that will meet their needs.

Take time to reflect on the implementation of best practices with technology, and determine what you need to do to incorporate these tools at your site. Figure 8.4 lists some ideas for the use of technology in schools.

WHAT ELSE CAN I DO?

In order to support your new teachers and create a climate where people want to work every day, take a look at what you are doing to build a positive decision-making school. Teacher-leaders within your building can

Figure 8.4 **Ideas to Support Technology in Schools**

Ideas to Support Technology in Schools	Suggested Actions
Use social media	Facebook, Twitter, blogs, discussion groups
Hold technology "how-to" sessions	Invite someone to model and teach how to use each piece of technology
Create classroom web pages, blogs, or wikis	Teacher/school designed to share successes and information
Use webquests to search for content information	Teacher-designed classroom activities
Use multimedia presentations	PowerPoint, Prezi, Keynote
E-mail	Principal-to-staff, teacher-to-parent-and-students, teacher-to-teacher
Use the Internet to help students search for information, video clips, and virtual tours	Teacher-led instruction on usage
Develop a series of podcasts	Teacher and student interactions
Use bring-your-own-device (BYOD) or onsite technology tools	Appropriate use in the classroom and school
Create a series of video streaming sessions	Teacher- and student-created
Play games using phones or mobile devices	Teacher and student interactions
Use video conferencing	National and international connections

provide everyone a chance to make a difference in the choices that are made in the best interest of the school community. You may never have 100% consensus, but having all educators participate in the instructional planning process leads to more involvement and participation in decisions that matter the most.

- Share your vision and mission for your learning teams. Develop a set of norms, roles, and responsibilities for consistency both vertically and horizontally across the school.

- Understand that everyone has a collective responsibility for all students.

- Have a designated place where teachers can meet, feel comfortable, and be uninterrupted.

- Create team- and grade-level professional learning communities or data teams.

- Develop and implement a set schedule for planning needs (instructional, logistical, data).

- Provide resources, websites, books, blogs, and material to support planning.

- Establish realistic SMART goals for areas in need of improving (achievement, attendance, behavior).

SELF-REFLECTION QUESTIONS

Take time to reflect on the questions in Figure 8.5 related to your role as a leader and your support of your new teachers. Your responses in both the strengths and challenges columns should help guide you with implementing strategies that will impact your school community. You should be able to chart your journey as the instructional leader as you progress through the year.

Figure 8.5   **Self-Reflection**

Reflection Questions	My Strengths	My Challenges	My Strategies
How do I manage communication within my building?			
How do I foster a decision-making culture in the school?			
How do we choose our priorities and determine realistic goals for our school?			
What kind of staff development have I provided to develop effective teaming?			

(Continued)

Figure 8.5 (Continued)

Reflection Questions	My Strengths	My Challenges	My Strategies
What are my teachers' perceptions about teaming?			
How do we analyze and interpret data so that instruction is changed to meet the needs of our students?			
How do I help my teacher-leaders by building capacity for everyone?			
How do I provide for uninterrupted planning time?			
How do I clearly define the roles and responsibilities of my team members?			
Do we have a planning model in place for vertical and horizontal planning teams? What can be improved with our process?			
How are team leaders selected, and what are their responsibilities to the team and to me?			
How do I assign teachers to teams?			

Effective Teaching and Best Practices

QUOTE

I could not believe it when I saw the lightbulb come on in their heads. It is true what they say that you can watch children learn and see how excited they get when they master a challenging task!

—First-year high school teacher

STORY FROM THE FIELD

There are so many things that new teachers do not know, and we tend to forget to tell them. Mr. Johnson began his career as a lateral entry teacher with a degree but no teaching experience in the classroom. He had more than 180 eighth-grade science students in a challenging environment and would admit that he was totally unprepared for the first year. His on-the-job training was enabling him to survive from day to day, but he needed a lot of help with his classroom organization and management. I met him during a walkthrough of the school and suggested that he attend one of our new teacher support seminars. The principal and I had a requirement that if new staff members were considering quitting, they had to give us a call first. Mr. Johnson was enthusiastic and wanted to be a great teacher. He remembered his high school teachers and college professors and was modeling his teaching style after these educators. He told his students that he would be taking up notebooks on Friday, grading each, and returning them on Monday.

On Sunday evening, he called me to say he had only completed the notebooks of his first period students, and he had six more classes' worth of notebooks to grade. I just told him to get some coffee brewing, and we would talk about this at our next new teacher seminar. I recognized that my new teachers were overwhelmed with day-to-day tasks and that effective teaching could not happen until we clearly defined strategies and methods.

THE ADMINISTRATOR'S ROLE

We often hear the terms *effective teachers* and *best practice*, but have we truly defined what they mean in the classroom? The phrase *best practice* has been used in the fields of medicine and law and describes state-of-the-art, solid work in a professional field. For you to help your new teachers implement best practices, you must be aware of the current research-based information and believe that the teaching profession has changed over the years. You may have educators on your staff who believe that what has worked for the past 20 years will continue to work. Consider the analogy of going to a physician who has not kept up with current research in medicine. I cannot imagine what the world would be like if we were not aware of the trends and innovations in the teaching profession. Today's schools have changed, and we should embrace this opportunity to reach the needs of a very diverse population of students.

Effective Teachers

Your school has effective teachers, and you know who they are. You would want your child in their classrooms and would do everything you could to get them there. Effective teachers continue to display certain characteristics over and over, and helping your new teachers understand these traits will improve all aspects of your school community.

Working with schools around the country, I have found several key factors that contribute to making teachers effective as instructional leaders and managers of their classrooms.

1. Effective teachers like the students they have.

Great teachers have a passion for teaching. If you do not see this passion in one of your new teachers, you will have to make a conscious decision to intervene. Teachers want to look forward to coming to work every day, and among the factors influencing the decision to intervene as a support, it is important to recognize the roller-coaster ride of feelings, emotions, and attitudes that teaching involves.

2. Effective teachers care about their students.

Intervention provides an opportunity for you to help support the relationship-building process between teacher and students. It takes time for teachers to get to know their students, especially in secondary school. There is a fine balance between being their teacher and being their friend. For many new and younger teachers, this will be something to continually work on during the year.

3. Effective teachers can relate to students.

Energy, dynamism, enthusiasm, and confidence are qualities that enable teachers to relate well to their students. I once told a teacher that I knew he really didn't like the students but that he "should act like it." Learning about what their students read, listen to, and play with, and about how they use technology to communicate, is important to building positive relationships. Effective teachers are just *cool* to their students.

4. Effective teachers are risk takers.

This is very difficult for new teachers to understand if they are not confident or secure in their teaching capacity. You will need to help them understand that teaching style is developed over time and that there is no one correct way to teach. What works for one teacher or one student is dependent on many factors.

5. Effective teachers know their content and how to deliver it in meaningful, relevant ways.

The walkthrough is a great time to determine if content knowledge is an issue with your new teachers. Some districts will hire new staff based just on a college degree and not on background or experience in education.

6. Effective teachers differentiate their teaching with multiple learning opportunities.

This includes the appropriate use of technology. If you have older generations of new teachers, they may have inadequate technology skills or may be unable to recognize learning differences. Supporting new teachers with multiple tools for classroom use will help them design better lessons.

Modeling Best Instructional Practices

When we talk about instructional practices, we need to look at the methods of the past and identify the needs of our students today. Because of the influx of technology, fast-paced media sources, and new visual and auditory cues, students learn differently than they did five years ago. In addition to being able to read nonfiction text, write in multiple formats, and do math and problem solving while communicating effectively, the learners of tomorrow will need a different set of skills.

The implications for the classroom are huge as teachers begin to understand their content and how best to present it to their students. Figure 9.1 outlines several suggested instructional practices that should be

Figure 9.1 **Suggested Best Practices**

Suggested Best Practices	What It Looks Like in the Classroom
Student-centered activities	
Teacher as facilitator	
Active learning with hands-on, experiential activities	
Differentiated instruction (Response to Intervention)	
Concept-based learning with Big Ideas and Essential Questions that guide instruction	
Flexible grouping	
Common formative assessments along with performance tasks	

Suggested Best Practices	What It Looks Like in the Classroom
Active movement and cooperative collaboration	
Discussions, shared responsibility, and accountability	
Open-ended, higher-level questions	
Hands-on, problem-based learning	
Nonfiction texts and real-world resources	
Choices for learning in content, process, and product	
Student self-reflection and assessment	

incorporated into daily and unit plans. As you read each, write a reflective statement on what your expectations will be when discussing these practices with your new staff.

WHAT ELSE CAN I DO?

It is important not only to recognize the traits of effective teachers and their instructional best practices but also to identify red flags in the classroom. Using walkthrough observations and guided feedback, you should be able to improve teaching and learning for all of your new staff. According to John Hattie (2009),

> The four types of instruction found to be most effective on teacher knowledge and behavior were: observation of actual classroom methods; microteaching; video-audio feedback; and practice. Lowest effects were from discussion, lectures, games/simulations, and guided field trips. Higher effect sizes were found in studies where: training groups involved both high school and elementary school teachers rather than only high or only elementary teachers; training programs were initiated, funded or developed by federal, state, government or university rather that by schools or teachers; participants were selected for trainings; and where training was practical rather than theoretical. (p. 120)

Here are some ideas for encouraging use of best practices among your new teachers:

- Define your description of an effective teacher, and share your expectations early in the year.

- Model a best instructional practice at a staff meeting. Allow time to share and discuss the implications for classrooms.

- Provide resources, book talks, and articles for learning how to differentiate instruction.

- Develop a professional development plan based on the needs of your new teachers.

- Use team meetings as a time for new and veteran teachers to share ideas and strategies.

SELF-REFLECTION QUESTIONS

Take time to reflect on the questions in Figure 9.2 related to your role as a leader and your support of your new teachers. Your responses in both the strengths and challenges columns should help guide you with implementing strategies that will impact your school community. You should be able to chart your journey as the instructional leader as you progress through the year.

Figure 9.2 **Self-Reflection Questions**

Reflection Questions	My Strengths	My Challenges	My Strategies
Have I defined the terms *effective teacher* and *best practice?*			
Have I helped new teachers reflect on what strategies work best for their students?			
What research have I shared with my new teachers to support their teaching styles?			
How do I encourage risk taking and innovative thinking?			
How do I hold teachers accountable for unit and lesson planning?			

(Continued)

Figure 9.2 **(Continued)**

Reflection Questions	My Strengths	My Challenges	My Strategies
Have I asked new teachers about their process or model for planning units of study and daily lessons?			
How do my teachers collaborate and team?			
Have I created protected team planning time?			
What areas do I need to help my teachers with to improve student achievement?			
What is our definition of differentiation? What support have I given my new teachers to meet the needs of all of our students?			

Observations
and Evaluations

QUOTE

If I only knew what the principal was looking for when he was in my room, I could just do it. I just don't have a clue.

—First-year teacher

STORY FROM THE FIELD

The fear of being observed by the principal or another administrator is so powerful that it actually makes new teachers ill. One of our new teachers I met recently had planned and stressed over her 45-minute lesson for weeks. She was a nervous wreck to think the principal was coming in to observe her class of 29 fifth-grade students. There had been no pre-evaluation conference or conversations prior to this formal visit, and it was early October. I could hear the fear in her voice the night before the observation, when she called around 11:00 p.m. All I could do was reassure her that she had planned and rehearsed well and that her students respected her greatly and would support her. The next day she called me and said that she had made it through without too many mistakes. The only issue was that she had misspelled the word *objective* on the board, but the principal never noticed the mistake. Her 29 students did, but they were very quiet about it.

THE ADMINISTRATOR'S ROLE

New teachers tell me that observations and evaluations are among the greatest causes of educational stress in their work. Induction programs typically do not communicate what teacher appraisal instruments expect and measure. Evaluations are conducted and filed without teachers being provided the skills and knowledge needed to effectively meet the requirements of the appraisal categories. Classroom walkthroughs are designed to be opportunities for growth rather than a "gotcha" situation. Observations made in the classroom are foundational to identifying effective teaching and instruction. It is important that principals allocate time to spend in every classroom in their buildings. If you are going to evaluate someone, then you must have the data and evidence to support your feedback.

There are several areas that the instructional leader must be thoroughly knowledgeable about before observing in classrooms:

1. Classroom management and positive behavior models

2. The curriculum standards

3. Methods for instruction and assessment

4. Interpersonal skills for communication and collaboration

Why Evaluate Teachers?

A useful evaluation process should provide teachers with feedback on their instructional presentations, use of time, class management, and organizational skills. The purpose of evaluations should be twofold: to measure teacher competence and ability, and to facilitate appropriate professional development and growth. A meaningful and purposeful evaluation should strike a balance between criticism and approval. The opportunity to learn strategies and make changes in the classroom should be the primary focus of observations. In addition, a chance to observe master teachers affords new teachers models of excellence as they develop their teaching and relationship styles with students.

The evaluation process follows a series of steps. First, a consensus on what to improve must be agreed on by both you and the teacher. There should be a reasonable goal that can be accomplished in a realistic time frame. Preconferences may provide a time for new teachers to tell you what they need to improve and what feedback they would like you to provide after your observation. Or postconferences may be the time when you actually identify issues and concerns and begin to draft a plan for improvement.

Second, once the goal is identified, determine the challenges for achieving it. This could include time, materials, resources, or the need for professional development.

Third, classroom observations should focus only on attaining this goal, and new teachers should focus on reaching it before choosing another.

New teachers cannot focus on too many tasks at once, and successful completion of one goal is better than frustration when too many are not accomplished.

Last, monitor the new teacher's progress, and celebrate success. New teachers like to hear that they are doing well, and motivation and morale will be stronger as encouragement becomes the norm for observations and evaluations.

Types of Evaluations and Observations

Evaluations and observations can be intimidating for both the administrator and the teacher. Established relationships, instructional knowledge, and expectations within the culture of the school are integral pieces that must be considered prior to evaluating teachers. While the building principal has a variety of duties, none is more important than helping new teachers learn how to manage, organize, and instruct in a classroom. It is imperative that the principal identify the specific needs in the new staff, as ignoring this or giving the duty to someone else will jeopardize not only the individual teachers' success but also the overall effectiveness of the school. Administrative leaders, instructional coaches, mentors, and support staff must establish a school culture that embraces positive and constructive feedback so that teaching and learning are improved.

Several of my favorite schools hold "instructional" staff meetings so that teachers can share best practices in areas such as classroom management, instructional techniques, and communication and collaboration strategies. Book talks related to staff needs are implemented along with gallery walks and round robin conversations. These are led by various staff members and provide a platform for discussions among all grade and content levels. These meetings provide new teachers with an opportunity to share their own experiences while learning from veteran teachers.

You must adopt an "I am not out to get you" tactic prior to completing any type of evaluation or observation. Take time to reflect on which of the following observation methods is most supportive for your new staff and how you inform them of your expectations.

Walkthrough

Tucker (2001) stated that whole-school improvement does not occur unless the instructional leader helps the teachers perform at a high-quality level. Cervone and Martinez-Miller (2007) described classroom walkthroughs as a tool to "drive a cycle of continuous improvement by *focusing on the effects of instruction*" (italics in original).

The tone and purpose of the instructional walkthrough is to build on what the teacher is doing well and what needs to be improved. The focus is on one or two dimensions of instruction, such as student engagement, standards, or management. Administrators establish themselves as the instructional leader as teams of observers focus on instruction, student motivation, and achievement.

Peer Observations

Peer observations involve having mentors, coaches, or other teachers assess and provide feedback related to an area of growth. Observers should meet with new teachers prior to visiting their classrooms and have a conversation around the strengths and challenges facing the new educator. It is suggested that only one or two improvement areas be targeted. It is important that the observer and the new teacher have an established, positive relationship prior to doing any evaluative recording. The observer's information is shared with both the teacher and the administrative team. One of our principals told me that she allowed her new teachers to "have a pass" to go and observe another teacher. Her only regret was that she offered it at any time during the year. Her suggestion is that this pass be used during the second half of the first quarter and not too late in the year.

Knight (2007) and Duncan (2006) have developed coaching models that support consulting and collaboration and have been implemented in numerous districts and schools. Arthur L. Costa and Robert J. Garmston (2002) established a process called *cognitive coaching* in which trust, learning, and growth are the focus for continual individual and collective improvement. Through the use of inquiry and questioning, educators are able to self-evaluate and reflect on their successes and challenges. Notes from observations are shared and focus on several key areas for growth. Peer observers are responsible for helping self-evaluating teachers to recognize the things that they are doing well and how to make adjustments through a nonjudgmental approach.

Informal and/or Unannounced Observations

Leaders who visit classrooms send a strong message of support. These informal visits require time and consistency in order to become part of the daily school routine. While there is no preconference for these observations, the focus is based on prior conversations or observations, teacher requests, and classroom visits by the administrative team. It is also important to note that these informal visits usually last 10–15 minutes and occur during different times of the day. These may be announced or unannounced, but the purpose is to provide a snapshot of one area of growth. Feedback can also be informal in the form of a note, e-mail, or brief conversation.

Formal and Announced Observations

Most districts have an established format for conducting formal observations of staff members. These observations should include a pre- and postconference between the leader and the teacher. These conferences provide the opportunity to share successes and challenges and identify growth areas as determined by other observations. These observations usually last for a class period or lesson and are conducted by a certified staff member. An observation report is prepared, and there is an established time for the teacher and observer to review the report together. Consensus on or rebuttal to the stated comments is added to the report after this meeting.

Tucker (2001) stated that the most difficult part of drafting a support plan for a new teacher is determining the exact problems to address. This is very true if you have a lot of issues and must determine which ones are at the top of the priority list. Building relationships is critical, and it is not enough to think you know good teaching. You must be able to clearly identify the small- and large-scale components that make up effective teaching.

New teachers may need support in a number of different categories related to effective teaching. Take time to reflect on the areas listed in Figure 10.1, and determine your priority in helping your new teachers improve their practices.

Figure 10.1 Areas of Growth and Reflective Practices

Areas of Growth	**Reflective Practices**
Classroom organization/time management	
Classroom management	
Relationship building	
Instructional delivery	

(Continued)

Figure 10.1 (Continued)

Areas of Growth	Reflective Practices
Instructional duties (required)	
Instructional duties (nonrequired)	
Planning and lesson design	
Standards and assessments	
Professional development	

Dr. Lena Marie Rockwood is a middle school assistant principal at the Rumney Marsh Academy in Revere Public Schools in Massachusetts. The school is located in an urban setting; approximately 75% of students receive free or reduced-price lunch, and multiple languages are spoken. As a veteran teacher and administrator, Rockwood is a member of the Revere Educators Leadership Board and has researched how to hire good teachers and retain them as part of the Recruitment, Hiring, and Placement Committee. The administrative team in the district has implemented an evaluation process in which teachers are able to complete a self-assessment and share their areas of growth. Teachers receive constructive feedback through a series of face-to-face and online conversations based on observations and collected data. The administrative team collaborates with all new teachers to discuss curriculum, teaching, parent/community involvement, and professional responsibilities. It is very clear when you talk with Rockwood that she has a passion for helping build capacity in her new staff members.

She asks questions to prompt thinking, and she has a sharing, not telling, philosophy when meeting with teachers. All teachers are given time to develop their own personal SMART goal, which focuses on two areas: professional practice and student learning. The feedback that teachers receive from Rockwood is constructive and positive, which allows everyone to be more reflective and encourages discussion in order to implement change where needed. One thing that is very clear to her is that the 40-minute dog-and-pony show that teachers put on during formal evaluations is not the reality of what actually happens in the classroom. The time she spends in classrooms every day allows her to have the whole picture of teaching and learning, so that teachers receive feedback on their day-to-day instruction that is helpful and meaningful and that fosters professional growth.

She says,

It is my job to support teachers and help them develop effective teaching strategies that positively impact student learning. I want my feedback to be supportive and productive in order to strengthen classroom practices. Timing is everything. We must find their shining moments and build on these.

Rockwood is in classrooms every day looking for ways to help new teachers focus on their one or two areas of improvement. One of the things that she notices is that new teachers want to be a friend to students, not the teacher, in the classroom. As a result, classroom management is one of the predominant areas that are discussed on a frequent basis. Rockwood knows that all new teachers will struggle, and she understands that many of them enter the profession with ideas about the classroom that are different from the reality. With that in mind, she makes it a priority to help new teachers transition into the classroom seamlessly.

The First Steps

The first step is finding those who need help and support. You must decide who is struggling the most and determine how you will help them. It is a very clear that most new teachers will not ask for help, or if they do, they don't know what to ask. Often they will confide in a mentor or colleague, as they perceive it a sign of weakness to go to the administration with concerns. And parents are always willing to share issues about new teachers, but they seldom go to the teacher in the beginning. I met with a group of 127 new teachers before the first week of school. I made the mistake of asking them, "What questions do you have?" The room was silent, but meeting with the same group after the first day allowed me to determine that they really didn't have a clue about teaching. All new teachers will struggle in some capacity. Even if the new teacher has completed student teaching or something similar, the culture of every school is different in regard to policies, procedures, and logistics. While dealing with first-year educators, consider that others in your building may need support as well, and creating a plan for them will help ensure school improvement. The philosophy in your building should be that we can *all* get better at what we do.

Teachers must know the content, understand how students learn, plan lessons that are engaging and level-appropriate, use a variety of instructional methods, and manage and evaluate the effectiveness of their daily lessons. If you want improvement to occur, you must be specific in your communication and expectations. We must also consider that individuals must see the need to change and have a reason for improvement. You just cannot tell them to improve; they must understand the why and how and what it means to them.

Fear of Administrators

I have found that many new teachers have a healthy fear of their administrators. They do not want to offend anyone, will often not speak out about concerns or issues, and do not know how to approach or talk to their administrator. All schools have a culture, whether it is a positive, collaborative climate or one in which a top-down, micromanagement approach is used.

Districts often have surveys, administered at the end of the year, that collect specific data to help find out what is needed for school improvement. Teachers, parents, and students are provided an opportunity to comment on how they think the school is working and on the successes and challenges experienced within the school setting. It is important for principals to have a handle on how things are going prior to the end of the year, as it is too late to make midcourse changes. Informal teacher surveys, such as the "How Am I Doing" Administrator Feedback Form shown in Figure 10.2, provide valuable information that administrators can use to inform instructional leadership decisions. The survey should be confidential and given to all teachers, not just your new staff.

Figure 10.2   "How Am I Doing" Administrator Feedback Form

Use the table below to rank the statements.

(5 = strongly agree, 4 = agree, 3 = no opinion, 2 = disagree, 1 = strongly disagree)

	5	4	3	2	1
My principal makes me feel comfortable when talking.					
My principal is available when I have confidential concerns.					
My principal listens to me.					
My principal respects me.					
My principal observes me fairly.					
My principal is accessible and visible.					
My principal respects my time.					
My principal shares best practices with me to help me become a better teacher.					
My principal allows me to share ideas and try new strategies.					
My principal provides positive and supportive feedback.					
My principal micromanages the staff.					
My principal allows for team collaboration and decision making.					
My principal creates a supportive and caring climate for all.					
I am very happy with my teaching position.					

Which of the following words best describe your relationship with your principal? Check all that apply.

- ❑ Trusting
- ❑ Supportive
- ❑ Caring
- ❑ Tense
- ❑ Respectful
- ❑ Micromanaging
- ❑ Bullying
- ❑ Compassionate
- ❑ Knowledgeable
- ❑ Hostile
- ❑ Friendly
- ❑ Threatening
- ❑ Dishonest
- ❑ Listening
- ❑ Problem solving

One resource that districts and school have used over the years is The New Teacher Center (NTC) in Santa Cruz, California. The center's focus is on accelerating the effectiveness of new teachers, thus improving student learning. States, school districts, and policymakers are able to partner with the NTC to design and implement processes that create sustainable, high-quality mentoring and professional development. In addition, leadership capacity, teacher working conditions, retention, and school transformation are critical areas of focus.

WHAT ELSE CAN I DO?

New teachers are afraid of making mistakes, especially if someone is watching. The level of trust and relationship that you have with them will determine their level of anxiety during formal observations.

- Put yourself in their shoes. Remember what it is liked to be evaluated by someone else.

- Begin with the positive.

- Provide descriptions, explanations, and specific examples of what is expected during classroom walkthroughs and formal observations. This should be done at the beginning of the year through written materials and team discussions.

- Never, ever leave a classroom without speaking to the teacher or leaving a note about something positive you observed.

- Talk with the students, and ask them "How is your teaching doing?"

- Review your relationship-building skills, and take time to improve if you are not as effective as you should be.

- Make your feedback specific, timely, accurate, and relevant.

- Establish times for a preconference and postconference to learn lesson objectives, class demographics, teaching methods, and other information. This is the opportunity for both parties to ask questions.

- Provide a set of guiding questions focused on specific evidence for teaching. Questions that you may use are found in Figure 10.3, Pre- and Postconference Question Suggestions; Figure 10.4, Preconference Planner; and Figure 10.5, Postconference Reflection.

- Ensure that all of your comments dignify the teacher and provide hope and encouragement.

- Be genuine but honest. Never, ever lie about a problem; state it in a way that support is provided.

- Visit a classroom just for fun and not for an evaluation. Tell the teacher that you will be doing this.

Figure 10.3 Pre- and Postconference Question Suggestions

Topic	Preconference Questions	Postconference Questions

General Questions	• What did you do prior to planning this lesson?
	• What do I need to know about your classroom and your students?
	• How do you anticipate your students will respond to the lesson?
	• What are your strengths and challenges?
	• What are your expectations for
	  ○ learning?
	  ○ behavior?
	  ○ instruction?
	• How have you been communicating with your parents about their students?
		• How are things going?
		• What results have you achieved up to now?
		• As you think about the lesson I observed, what aspect or part of it do you think was the most effective? What evidence do you have for your answer?
		• As the lesson progressed, did you make any changes to your instruction? Why or why not?
		• Did you achieve your stated learning outcomes? How do you know?
		• What have you learned from this lesson or others that will affect your planning for future lessons, in terms of either improving your own instructional skills or addressing students' instructional needs?
		• If you were to teach this lesson again, would you do anything differently? If so, why?
		• Think about your professional growth. What areas are your strengths, and what areas are in your improvement goals?
		• What are your thoughts about the feedback from this observation?
		• What did you learn from this lesson that you will use the next time you work with this class?

Classroom Environment	• How does the arrangement of your classroom facilitate learning? • How do you model respect for learning and each student? • How is safety addressed during your lesson?	• Is there anything you would change about your classroom? How can I help with this? • What else you do need to know about safety for your students? • What are your concerns about movement in your room?

(Continued)

Figure 10.3 (Continued)

Topic	Preconference Questions	Postconference Questions
Classroom Management	• Are there any students about whom you have concerns? What are they? • What should I know about this particular class in regard to behavior? • Is this a grade-level appropriate lesson?	• What do you need help with in regard to management strategies? • Is there a particular student who needs attention?
Instructional Planning	• What do you think will be the most effective thing you do in helping students learn this lesson? • What evidence do you have for your decisions? • What learning outcomes are intended for the lesson? • How did you assess students' prior knowledge before beginning the lesson? • How does the lesson connect to real-world experiences for your students? • What is the focus or objective of the lesson? How did you share this with the students? • What standards are addressed in the planned instruction? • What do you want students to know and be able to do by the end of this lesson? • Why is this learning important? • How did you choose the lesson format? What knowledge of your students informed your decision? Did you decide on the format based on your knowledge of your students? • What instructional strategies and methods will be used to engage students and promote independent learning and problem solving?	• What were the strengths in this lesson? What were the challenges? How do you know? • Did you choose the best learning outcome? • Would you change the way you shared the objective with your students? Why or why not? • How successful were your students? • How will you adapt future instruction based on your assessment of student learning in this lesson? • Did your students understand the connection to the real-world examples? • Which strategies worked, and which did not? How do you know? • Were all of your students engaged? How do you know?

Topic	Preconference Questions	Postconference Questions
Instruction and Assessment	• How did you assess prior learning and knowledge? • How do you know your students learned the information presented? • Is this lesson grade-level appropriate? How do you know? • Are the tasks aligned with the standard's skills and content? • How will you know that your students are learning? What type of assessment will you use? • What formal and informal assessment strategies will you use? • What do you want your students to give you to show they understand the content and objective of the lesson? • What self-reflection strategies will your students use? • How will you use assessment data from this lesson to reteach or enrich the next lesson? Develop the next lesson?	• How do you know your students were engaged in learning? • How do you know they learned what you were teaching? • What affect did your assessments have on student learning? • Would you change the outcome of the lesson by changing what you ask students to accomplish? • How effective is the students' self-reflection? How would you change this? • What are your next growth steps?
Differentiating	• Can all the students do the work you are presenting? If not, how will you meet the learning needs of all of your students in this class? • What do you know about your students that allows you to adjust instruction? • How will the instructional strategies address all students' learning needs? • How will the lesson engage and challenge students of all levels? • How will developmental gaps be addressed?	• What was the benefit of using differentiation with your students? • Did your lesson meet the needs of all of your students? Why or why not? • Do you need additional support for learning to differentiate? • What kind of support can I provide to help with the diverse population of students?
Resources	• What resources and materials will be used in the lesson? • Is there anything you need prior to teaching this lesson? • Will technology be integrated into this lesson? How and why?	• Did the resources support your lesson? • Is there anything else you need with materials or resources? • How can I support your use of technology in this class?
Collaboration and Communication	• Did you share your planning with your mentor or a colleague? • How do you reflect on your teaching each day?	• How supportive is your assigned mentor/colleague? What else can I do to help with teaming and collaboration? • What else can I do?

Figure 10.4 **Preconference Planner**

Teacher	Date/Time
Observer	
Standard(s)	
Objective	
Number of students	
Accommodations needed	
Challenge areas	
Resources used	
Strategy(ies) used in lesson	
Focus/growth area targeted	
Assessment strategy used	
Differentiation (if needed)	
Summarization and self-reflection	
Postconference date and time	

Figure 10.5   Postconference Reflection

Teacher	Date/Time
Observer	
How do you think the lesson went and why?	
What were the strengths and weaknesses of this lesson?	
How do you know your students met the learning goal?	
How did the lesson align with your focus standard?	
How did the lesson strategies engage the students before, during, and after the lesson?	
What strategy was the most effective? Which would you change?	
What resources did you find the most useful during the lesson? Do you need anything else?	
How did data inform the teaching of this lesson?	
How did your assessment strategies inform your instruction?	
Did you have fun teaching this lesson? Why or why not?	

SELF-REFLECTION QUESTIONS

Take time to reflect on the questions in Figure 10.6 related to your role as a leader and your support of your new teachers. Your responses in both the strengths and challenges columns should help guide you with implementing strategies that will impact your school community. You should be able to chart your journey as the instructional leader as you progress through the year.

Figure 10.6 Self-Reflection Questions

Reflection Questions	My Strengths	My Challenges	My Strategies
How do I identify the strengths and challenges of my new teachers?			
How have I shared my vision and mission for effective teaching?			
How have I shared the instrument I use to evaluate teachers?			
How do I identify the skills that my new teachers need to work on first?			
Do I provide time for my new teachers to observe my master teachers?			

Reflection Questions	My Strengths	My Challenges	My Strategies
How do I conduct pre- and postconferences before and after formal evaluations?			
What tangible reinforcement do I provide for new teachers?			
What type of feedback do I provide to enable growth and learning?			
What does my body language say during conferences and classroom visits?			
What have my students said about their teachers that would allow me to inform the teachers of growth areas?			

Celebrating Success

STORY FROM THE FIELD

Working with new teachers over the years has been very rewarding. After spending a year with about 200 beginning educators and their principals, I realized that it really was the small things that made a difference. One of my new social studies teachers called me on a workday after school was out and asked if I would visit his classroom. He invited his principal and me to his room and showed us the inside door of his tall file cabinet. On it he had taped all of the seminar invitations and sticky notes that we both had left him during the year. He told us that when he was frustrated and wanted to quit, he would just open this door and see a very colorful display that reflected how we both needed him to be at school every day.

What are you doing to celebrate success in your school?

THE ADMINISTRATOR'S ROLE

Scenarios like the one above are not uncommon with new teachers. With all of the challenges and issues facing them on a day to day basis, many want to hold on to small tokens of recognition and appreciation. Although the sticky notes were simple, each one sent a powerful message that this teacher, and all teachers, were valued for what they did in their classrooms. The feedback provided was respectful and dignified and offered only one suggestion at a time. Improvement happens over the span of months, and this teacher was able to track his growth and celebrate success.

People celebrate success in different ways. We recognize students, teachers, and community members who contribute to the overall improvement of their school. Achievement in academics, citizenship, behavior, and attendance are just a few of the many successes that are celebrated during the year. It is important to note that while we think it natural to celebrate our students' successes, we need to make a conscious effort to celebrate the successes of our teaching staffs as well. When our educators are recognized for their hard work, their sense of satisfaction translates into high morale and motivation throughout the building. Happy teachers make learning more engaging for students. All principals want their teachers to be exemplary, improve student achievement, and continue to enjoy coming to work each day. Their job is easier when they have experienced educators in the building. But when they have new teachers as well, recognizing success takes time and effort on a daily basis. Effective principals know that when teacher quality improves, student improvement will naturally occur.

Why Celebrate?

Have you ever wondered why we celebrate? In a list of all the things you celebrate, you might include birthdays, weddings, the birth of a child, sporting events, holidays, pay raises, a new house or car, and the list goes on. I want you to think about something you have done recently that gave you a great sense of pride in your accomplishment. This could be a personal or professional triumph. What did you do? Did you tell someone? Could you hardly wait to share the achievement? What was the reaction of others?

The world has celebrated success since the beginning of time. Teams and organizations that focus on and celebrate success will always create positive environments for their employees. We, as a culture, expect this, and our behaviors and habits are created and developed based on our positive and negative actions. One of my new teachers told me about his parents. As a child, every night before he went to bed, his parents would ask him what he had done well during the day. He told me that he often had to think really hard about the question, but sometimes the answer came easily. This action was carried over into his classroom as he began his first year of teaching. At the end of every period, he would have his students think about one good thing that they had done since getting up that morning. Sometimes they would share, and other times they would just reflect. The culture in his classroom was so positive that parents began asking to have their children in his room.

Recall Ynez Olshausen from Chapter 1. She is an extraordinary leader at a school where international culture and global awareness is the theme. She puts her staff and students first in every way possible. Her presence in the building is strong, and she is well respected and appreciated by everyone in her school community. She knows that faculty and staff motivation is critical to teacher and student performance, positive school culture, and a productive environment. I have often heard her ask what school celebration sounds and looks like, with a focus on always having an open door policy for communication and collaboration. At staff meetings, she does at least one celebration a month and gives out colored globes to recognize special achievements. Each administrator does a "You Mean the World to Me" award and gives out apples to teachers who do extraordinary things. Teachers give out the "Uncommon Core" award to celebrate each other in regard to teaching and learning the new standards.

WHAT ELSE CAN I DO?

Teacher appreciation should be evident more often than just during a specific week in the school year. It should be the norm of a school building, and time should be provided frequently to share the good things that are going on. After spending considerable time in schools and classrooms, I have collected a set of suggestions that you may consider to show your teachers that you really care about them. It is not the size of your budget that counts; the amount of compassion and consideration for what your teachers do is more important.

- Give a thank-you, and do it often. This could be a verbal comment or a note in a teacher's box. Did you know that Doug Conant, the CEO of Campbell's Soup, has written 16,000 thank-you notes to employees since 2001 and reenergized the company in the process?

- Provide specific praise. You can do this in private, at a team or staff meeting, in writing, or any time that you are walking the halls.

- Recognize teachers and their classes on the morning or afternoon announcements. If you are in a challenging school, find small successes, such as 100% attendance by both students and teacher on a daily basis.

- Provide treats and snacks. Food is a great motivator, and monthly treats with a quote or motivational saying are fun for teachers to find in their boxes in the morning.

- Put a blue ribbon award that states a specific success on a classroom door. This could be for attendance, achievement, or behavior. Teachers get excited when their students can be showcased for the hard work done by all.

- Put a sticky note with words of appreciation on teachers' desks after you visit their classrooms. I did this consistently for my new teachers, and at the end of the year, one of them showed me every single note that I had written. They covered her desk.

- Ask teachers for advice on something. Asking for their suggestions shows that you value their personal contributions to the success of the school.

- Smile! It may be one of the most difficult tasks you ever have, but a friendly face (if you are truly genuine) never turns people off. Ask your teachers what you can do for them, not just how they are doing.

- Plan the workroom bulletin boards with care. What can you display that will show you care about your staff and who they are as people?

- Talk to everyone in the building, including bus drivers and cafeteria, custodial, and maintenance staff. You want to model that you appreciate the efforts of all. One of my favorite principals volunteered to help out in the lunch line until he was told that it was a violation of a food safety code. He moved from behind the counter to become the "greeter" for the lunch line.

- Provide social and fun time at staff meetings. Recognize the positive in your staff. One of my principals had the "Golden Giraffe" award for incredible accomplishments each month. I really don't know why they had a giraffe, but it was a large, stuffed, carnival-type animal that all the teachers wanted to have to display in their room.

- Sit in on a class, and participate with the students. As the leader of the school, you are looked at as the principal, but students need to see you as a learner.

- Host a thank-you breakfast when it is least expected. February is always a miserable month for new teachers. One of my schools had food, foot massagers, and bottle of bubbles for the teachers, so they could just play and have a bit of fun.

- In the spring, after a really cold winter, put a bouquet of flowers in the workroom to celebrate the coming of warmer weather.

- Provide a "Cafeteria Cookie/Treat" coupon for teachers to redeem during their lunch period.

- At staff meetings, have an "I'll cover your class" drawing once a month. This will give your new teachers a chance to take a break, observe a master teacher, or just catch up on paperwork. Just have this arranged in advance, so that this time can be covered by someone else in the building.

- If allowed or wanted, recognize teacher birthdays during the year. A cupcake is always a welcome treat along with a card celebrating the day.

- Purchase a special, motivational book for the school media center in honor of the accomplishments of one of your new teachers. Write the teacher's name, the date, and the great deed inside the book, and dedicate it during a staff meeting.

- Take individual photos (with permission) of your new teachers. Make a framed copy with a special quote or thank-you for each new teacher, and give them the photos at the end of the year.

SELF-REFLECTION QUESTIONS

Take time to reflect on the questions in Figure 11.1 related to your role as a leader and your support of your new teachers. Your responses in both the strengths and challenges columns should help guide you with implementing strategies that will impact your school community. You should be able to chart your journey as the instructional leader as you progress through the year.

The leaders described in this book have contributed to helping you learn and implement strategies that will help you support and retain your new staff members. Many of these leaders have spent years perfecting their relationships, building capacity for teaching and learning, and creating positive environments in which everyone in their building succeeds. Their stories are real and from the heart. I often look at these leaders as those who have come through the trenches but still remember what it was like to be a first-year teacher. Those who don't forget will continue to refine and review their leadership styles and the qualities that make for high-achieving schools.

I think of you, our instructional leaders, as analogous to SCUBA-diving instructors. You are given a diverse group of participants, some inexperienced, and some who have had practice, and you prepare to put them into a pool. Most of them have seen pictures or videos of diving, and it really looks quite easy. Some have a fear of the water, and some love it. There is a lot of equipment, and it must all be working before the group submerges. The instructions are complex and often confusing, especially to those who might not speak the SCUBA language. All the participants are learning at their own rate, whether with a ready-to-go or a wait-and-let-me-think-about-it approach. There is a test at the end, and it determines whether each participant passes or fails. And once they actually get into the water, there are creatures that approach them, in a variety of sizes, shapes, and confrontation modes. How they react to these may determine whether they survive or not.

Although this is just an analogy, you must take into consideration the impact that you have on the retention of teachers. What you do will make a difference in the end in creating educators that celebrate their success with you.

Figure 11.1 **Self-Reflection Questions**

Reflection Questions	My Strengths	My Challenges	My Strategies
What did I find the most challenging while supporting my new teachers?			
What did I do this year to support my new teachers?			
What was the most important thing I learned this year?			
How am I genuine and sincere when it comes to appreciating my new teachers?			
How do I show appreciation for my new staff members?			

Reflection Questions	My Strengths	My Challenges	My Strategies
What did I do differently for my new teachers to show that I care about their work?			
What do I want to celebrate at my school?			
What kind of recognition did I give my new teachers at the end of the year?			
How did my actions impact the retention of my new teachers?			

Final Thoughts

The world of education is challenging and full of constant change. Administrators, especially the building principal, have the opportunity to make or break their new teachers. As you reflect on your years in education, take time to consider what you do to support and nurture your beginning staff members. What you do on a regular basis will build the skills and knowledge needed for teachers to impact student achievement. The stories and strategies in this book suggest great starting places for you to begin to make the difference.

It is important to talk about the realities of today's classroom. The list below is compiled from multiple "aha" moments reflecting what new teachers wish they had known before the start of school. Although the comments seem simple to us reading them, they reflect a need to share real stories and scenarios early in the year. Use them as starting points for discussion; they will help ensure that you are doing everything you can to prepare your new staff for the first day and many years thereafter.

- Kindergarten boys like to have peeing contests in the bathroom.
- Children are abused and neglected by their family members.
- Students carry weapons, and people do bad things.
- Teachers get sick. Students get sick. All come to school.
- Some students have good hygiene practices, but many do not.
- Teachers have to report child abuse.
- Lockdowns happen for a reason.
- Mistakes are okay and are learning opportunities.
- Boys fight; girls fight differently.
- You should stock up on disinfectant cloths and wipes.
- Teachers fall in classrooms.
- Teachable moments happen. Take advantage of them.
- Velcro is better in kindergarten than zippers.
- Everyone likes recognition and praise.

- Students can't read.

- Some teachers can't do higher-level math.

- The school secretary is really, really important.

- Always, always have assigned seats on the first day.

- Your first year of teaching is your worst. It does get better.

The life of an educator lacks predictability. There is no one solution to solve the problem of teacher retention, but assessing your strengths and challenges and implementing a plan of action will determine whether you retain or recruit. All new teachers deserve support systems and processes that enable them to become great educators. It is your responsibility to provide the lead for their success. I wish you the best and hope for continued support with your new teachers.

References and Suggested Readings

Ainsworth, L. (2001). *Rigorous curriculum design: How to create curricular units of study that align standards, instruction, and assessment.* Englewood, CO: Advanced Learning Press.

Black, P. J., & Wiliam, D. (2009). Developing the theory of formative assessment. *Educational Assessment, Evaluation and Accountability, 21*(1), 5–31.

Borko, H. (2004). Professional development and teacher learning: Mapping the terrain. *Educational Researcher, 33*(8), 3–15.

Cervone, L., & Martinez-Miller, P. (2007). Classroom walkthroughs as a catalyst for school improvement. *Leadership Compass, 4*(4), 1–4. Retrieved from http:// www.naesp.org/resources/2/Leadership_Compass/2007/LC2007v4n4a2 .pdf

Costa, A. L., & Garmston, R. J. (2002). *Cognitive coaching: A foundation for renaissance schools* (2nd ed.). Norwood, MA: Christopher-Gordon Publishers.

Darling-Hammond, L., & McLaughlin, M. W. (1995). Policies that support professional development in an era of reform. *Phi Delta Kappan, 76*(8), 597–604.

Davis, B., & Bloom, G. (1998). Support for new teachers. *Thrust for Educational Leadership, 28*(2), 16–18.

Delpit, L. D., & Dowdy, J. K. (2002). *The skin that we speak: Thoughts on language and culture in the classroom.* New York, NY: New Press.

Duncan, M. (2006). *Literacy coaching: Developing effective teachers through instructional dialogue.* Katonah, NY: Richard C. Owen.

Fletcher, S., & Villar, A. (2005, January). *Research on student achievement and the benefit-cost analysis of new teacher induction.* New Teacher Center at University of Santa Cruz, Seventh National Symposium—"Discover the Power of Teacher Induction," Fairmont Hotel, San Jose, CA.

Goldrick, L., Osta, D., Barlin, D., & Burn, J. (2012). *Review of state policies on teacher induction.* Santa Cruz, CA: New Teacher Center. Retrieved from http://www .newteachercenter.org

Hattie, J. (2009). *Visible learning: A synthesis of over 800 meta-analyses relating to achievement.* New York, NY: Routledge.

Howard, L. (2006). *Ready for anything: Supporting new teachers for success.* Englewood, CO: Lead + Learn Press.

Howard, L. (2010). *Five easy steps to a balanced science program.* Englewood, CO: Advanced Learning Press.

Howe, N., & Strauss, W. (2003). *Millennials go to college: Strategies for a new generation on campus.* Washington, DC: American Association of Collegiate Registrars and Admission Officers.

Knight, L. (2007). *Instructional coaching: A partnership approach to improving instruction.* Thousand Oaks, CA: Corwin.

Kriete, R. (2014). *The morning meeting book* (3rd ed.). Turners Falls, MA: Northeast Foundation for Children.

Lambert, L. (2006, May 9). Half of teachers quit in 5 years. *The Washington Post.* Retrieved from http://www.washingtonpost.com/wp-dyn/content/article/2006/05/08/AR2006050801344.html

Leahy, S., & Wiliam, D. (2009). *Embedding assessment for learning—a professional development pack.* London, UK: Specialist Schools and Academies Trust. Retrieved from www.dylanwiliam.org

Learning Forward. (2011). *Standards for professional learning.* Oxford, OH: Learning Forward. Retrieved from http://learningforward.org/standards-for-professional-learning

Leithwood, K., Louis, K. S., Anderson, S., & Wahlstrom, K. (2004). *Review of research: How leadership influences student learning.* Minneapolis, MN: Center for Applied Research and Educational Improvement, University of Minnesota. Retrieved from http://www.wallacefoundation.org/knowledge-center/school-leadership/key-research/Documents/How-Leadership-Influences-Student-Learning.pdf

Louis, K. S., Leithwood, K., Wahlstrom, K. L., & Anderson, S. E. (2010). *Learning from leadership: Investigating the links to improved student learning.* Toronto, ON: Center for Applied Research and Educational Improvement. Retrieved from http://www.wallacefoundation.org/knowledge-center/school-leadership/key-research/Pages/Investigating-the-Links-to-Improved-Student-Learning.aspx

Marzano, R. J. (2003). *Classroom management that works.* Alexandria, VA: ASCD.

Marzano, R. J., Pickering, D. J., & Pollock, J. E. (2001). *Classroom instruction that works.* Alexandria, VA: ASCD.

Marzano, R. J., Waters, T., & McNulty, B. (2005). *School leadership that works: From research to results.* Alexandria, VA: ASCD.

MetLife. (2013). *The MetLife survey of the American teacher: Challenges for school leadership.* Retrieved from https://www.metlife.com/assets/cao/foundation/MetLife-Teacher-Survey-2012.pdf

Moir, E. (2011). *Phases of first year teaching.* Retrieved from http://www.newteacher center.org/blog/phases-first-year-teaching

National Commission on Teaching and America's Future. (2007). *The high cost of teacher turnover.* Santa Cruz, CA: New Teacher Center. Retrieved from http://www.newteachercenter.org/contact

National Comprehensive Center for Teacher Quality. (2010). *Teacher preparation data tool.* Retrieved from http://www.teachingquality.org/sites/default/files

North Carolina Teacher Working Conditions Initiative. (2013). *Listening to North Carolina educator's general trends.* Retrieved from http://2012.ncteachingconditions.org/sites/default/files/attachments/NC12_report_general_trends.pdf

The Partnership for 21st Century Skills. (n.d.). *Framework for 21st century learning.* Retrieved from http://www.p21.org/our-work/p21-framework

Public Education Network (PEN). (2003). *The voice of the new teacher.* Washington, DC: Author. Retrieved from http://www.publiceducation.org/pdf/Publications/Teacher_Quality/Voice_of_the_New_Teacher.pdf

Reynolds, A. (1995). The knowledge base for beginning teachers: Education professionals' expectations versus research findings on learning to teach. *The Elementary School Journal, 95*(3), 199–221.

Rockoff, J. E. (2004). The impact of individual teachers on student achievement: Evidence from panel data. *American Economic Review, 94*(2), 247–252.

Sanders, N., & Kearney, K. (2008). *Performance expectations and indicators for education leaders: An ISLLC-based guide to implementing leader standards and a companion guide to the educational leadership policy standards.* Washington, DC: Council of Chief State School Officers. Retrieved from http://www.ccsso.org

Seidel, A. (2014). *The teacher dropout crisis* [Blog post]. Retrieved from http://www.npr.org/blogs/ed/2014/07/18/332343240/the-teacher-dropout-crisis

Tucker, P. (2001). Helping struggling teachers. *Educational Leadership, 58*(5), 52–55.

U.S. Department of Education. (2007). *Teacher attrition and mobility: Results from the 2004–05 teacher follow-up survey* (NCES 2007–307). Washington, DC: U.S. Government Printing Office.

The Wallace Foundation. (2013). *The school principal as leader: Guiding schools to better teaching and learning.* Retrieved from http://www.wallacefoundation.org/knowledge-center/school-leadership/effective-principal-leadership/Documents/The-School-Principal-as-Leader-Guiding-Schools-to-Better-Teaching-and-Learning-2nd-Ed.pdf

Whitaker, T. (2011). *What great teachers do differently: 17 things that matter most* (2nd ed.). London, UK: Routledge/Taylor & Francis.

Wiggins, G., & McTighe, J. (2005). *Understanding by design.* Alexandria, VA: ASCD.

Index

A SAGE Company

Helping educators make the greatest impact

CORWIN HAS ONE MISSION: to enhance education through intentional professional learning.

We build long-term relationships with our authors, educators, clients, and associations who partner with us to develop and continuously improve the best evidence-based practices that establish and support lifelong learning.